D0989904

The 28th of Iyar

The 28th of Iyar

*The dramatic,
day-by-day journal
of an American family
in Israel during the
Six Day War*

by EMANUEL FELDMAN

FELDHEIM PUBLISHERS
JERUSALEM   NEW YORK

Originally published by Bloch Publishing Company, 1968

ISBN 978-1-68025-294-1

Typesetting: Eden Chachamtzedek

PUBLISHED BY:
Feldheim Publishers
POB 43163 / Jerusalem, Israel

208 Airport Executive Park
Nanuet, NY 10954
www.feldheim.com

DISTRIBUTED IN EUROPE BY:
Lehmanns
+44-0-191-430-0333
info@lehmanns.co.uk
www.lehmanns.co.uk

DISTRIBUTED IN AUSTRALIA BY:
Golds World of Judaica
+613 95278775
info@golds.com.au
www.golds.com.au

Printed in Israel

A virtuous wife is her
husband's crown...

MISHLEI 12:4

For Estelle

and **Ilan Daniel, Yisroel Yonatan,
Amram Hillel, Chavah Orah**,
who were there and who remember,
and **Geulah Batya**,
who was there but does not remember.

Other books by Emanuel Feldman

Jewish Law as Theology
The Biblical Echo
On Judaism
Tales out of Shul
One Plus One Equals One
The Shul without a Clock
Biblical Questions, Spiritual Journeys
Tales out of Jerusalem

... for Hashem has comforted His people,
He has redeemed Jerusalem.

YESHAYAHU 52:9

PROLOGUE:
Fear and Euphoria

IF A THOUSAND YEARS are, in G-d's eyes, like a single yesterday (*Tehillim* 90:4), how much more insignificant, in His eyes, is the span of a mere fifty years. Certainly in terms of Jewish history, such a period is barely a speck on the screen of time.

And yet, the past fifty years in the State of Israel — between 1967, the year of the Six Day War during which this book was written, and 2017— seem like several lifetimes.

In 1967, the lightning victory of the war against our Arab enemies was so swift that we were certain that we were hearing the footsteps of Mashiach. The sense that something transcendent had occurred, that we had been touched by the finger of G-d, was palpable and alive.

Now, fifty years later, while we still yearn for Mashiach, we have to strain to hear his footsteps. The wave of spirituality and piety that swept the country in 1967 has clearly dissipated. Similarly, the awe and admiration of the world toward the little David who rose up to defeat the mighty Arab Goliaths in 1967 has been transformed, by 2017, into an implacable world-wide anti-Semitism that views the Jewish state as the source of all evil.

And yet, in a kind of hidden miracle, Israel has continued to move forward. Physically, it is an economic powerhouse, one of the high-tech capitals of the world. Spiritually, serious Torah study and learning has never been more widespread. Problems and crises remain part of the daily menu, but for those who look beneath the surface, the guiding hand of the Creator is visibly at the helm.

Why reissue this memoir of the Six Day War now? Primarily, because that war was not just another war, to be relegated to the dust bins of history. At the onset of June, 1967, the State of Israel was a tiny strip of land along the Mediterranean coast. Six days later Israel was on the banks of both the Suez and the Jordan, the Sinai was in our hands, as was the Negev, as was the Golan, as was all of Yerushalayim, as was the Western Wall. Were we brutal conquerors, as per the current world narrative? Or was some mysterious Power at work here? This unembellished memoir of fear and euphoria enables readers to arrive at their own conclusions.

My appreciation to Feldheim Publishers for having the vision to reissue this volume in the hope that it will serve to uplift and inspire a generation that did not have the privilege to be there the first time.

Emanuel Feldman
Jerusalem
5777/2017

PREFACE

OF THE MAKING OF books about the Six Day War in Israel there is no end: so might King Shlomo, were he alive today, have written (*Koheles* 12:12). Why, then, still another book?

Because this is not a book in the ordinary sense of plan and outline and plot, but a day-by-day journal in which are recorded the emotions and moods and sights and sounds of a people hovering on the brink of disaster and, in the space of sixty sudden hours, soaring on the wings of triumph.

This is an intimate, personal, subjective account. As is the case with any diary, it makes no claims to Olympian detachment, and was in fact not originally written to be published. But during the months following the war it became evident that, while there was a surfeit of books dealing with the military strategy, the battlefield heroics, and the political machinations behind the war, nothing was being said to help understand and record the story of the Israeli on the home front and his reactions to the crisis, the danger, the war, and the victory: his moments of agony, despair, fear, and anxiety as well as joy, hope, laughter, and fulfillment.

This tale of ordinary human beings caught up in a net of international power intrigue is a significant one and deserves some documentation. This I have attempted to do in this modest journal, which was written on the spot as the story unfolded during those frantic days and nights in May and June 1967.

It is presented now as it was written then, with only minor changes. Hopefully, any literary and stylistic shortcomings will be compensated for by the retention of the original flavor and mood. With occasional exceptions, I have concealed the identity and changed the names of close friends and neighbors who appear in these pages.

Only a happy stroke of circumstance enabled my wife and me and our four children (now, thank God, increased to five) to be in Israel during this dramatic period: we were granted a sabbatical year after having served Atlanta's Congregation Beth Jacob since 1952, and for the academic year we lived in Israel where I was a guest lecturer at Bar Ilan University.

The officers and members of the congregation, therefore, have a share in this work, and to them I extend sincere appreciation. Special acknowledgments are also due to Mrs. Sylvia Held and to Mrs. Jackie Hirsch for their graciousness and devotion in typing a large portion of the manuscript.

It would be impossible to adequately express my indebtedness to my wife who contributes so much in so many direct and subtle ways to all that I write and do.

And, of course, our gratitude goes out to the God of Israel who kept us in life to experience the twenty-eighth day of *Iyar*, 5727, when His people was comforted and Jerusalem redeemed.

Emanuel Feldman
Atlanta, Georgia
5727/1967

8 Iyar

Thursday, May 18

THE PRESSURE IS BUILDING. Every page of every newspaper is thick with rumors and theories and speculation: Nasser is bluffing, Nasser is not bluffing; the U.N. will save the situation, the U.N. is useless; Israel should retaliate now, Israel should wait. Wherever you go the people ask, *"Mah yihyeh* — What will be?" At the university in which I lecture, students no longer study but spend their time wondering and worrying if they will be called up — or if their brothers and fathers will be called up. Even the most sanguine among the Israelis is caught up in the general gloom.

We have come here for only a year, and are due to leave in a few weeks. The year has been eventful: lecturing, writing, studying, learning the country and the language. But now, suddenly, a creeping spiritual paralysis has set in. There is endless tension: a wild compulsion to hear every news broadcast, to carry the transistor wherever I go; sitting and thinking about what to do and what will be; frustration and helplessness, and the inability to read, or study, or think, or lecture, or relax. Wouldn't it be nice (nice is the wrong word, it just occurred to me) simply to record — and to record simply — just what is happening each day: thoughts, fears, apprehensions, worries, rumors, reflections, speculations, conversations, theories. It should be of interest to me in the future to read about these things the way they happened. Already the wild rumors and cockeyed theories we hear on the streets are beginning to blur reality. It may be helpful someday to know what actually did occur. And a practical benefit is that writing things down at the end of each day will do much toward keeping me sane.

Is it possible that just forty-eight hours ago we were at the Independence Day parade in Jerusalem? We all got up at four A.M., drove into Tel Aviv, took a special train to Jerusalem, laughed with the revelers who had been up all night and were now on the way to the parade with us. I wondered, as I watched them celebrate, if they knew what this day was all about, and I worried that these Independence Day celebrations might someday become nothing more than a Middle Eastern Fourth of July. But the train ride up to Jerusalem was too beautiful, the sky too azure, the mountains too exhilarating for us to worry about such mundane matters.

We arrived in Jerusalem at eight. (I still can't comprehend the easy glibness with which we come and go into Jerusalem. Jerusalem! Avraham our Patriarch, Kings David and Shlomo, all went to Jerusalem — and we go to Jerusalem.)

We walked to the parade route, found a nice spot along the street, dragged over some bricks and planks from a construction site, and erected a grandstand seat for the six of us right there at the curb. And the parade: modest this year because of international pressures on Jerusalem. No tanks, no planes, no large pieces of military equipment. The soldiers so young, so serious, so shy, so self-conscious. Some of them tried to look straight ahead, but their curiosity got the better of them and their eyes darted to the side, stealing a brief glance at the crowd. And the crowd itself was so festive, the Yemenite women chortling their greetings like birds — *hoooohy* — and dressed as always in their dazzling yellow and blue and green.

After the parade we walked down towards *Har Tzion* and the Jordanian border. On the old wall, Jordanian soldiers silently patrolling. Watching the parade?

It was a pleasant time in Jerusalem two days ago. That night at home, on the spur of the moment, I wrote a long letter to my folks in the United States about my parade thoughts and about Zechariah's prophecy (4:6) "Not by might and not by power, but by My spirit, says Hashem." The sentiments in the letter were noble, I suppose, and certainly true. But by the next morning there seemed to be more power and more might and less spirit than ever, and my letter seemed rather hollow. Egypt announced with great fanfare that she was massing her troops in the Sinai desert. She also demanded that the UN pull out her peace-keeping troops. It sounded like the usual Egyptian bluff and bluster, but the situation was more threatening than usual.

Last night I met our neighbor Sheinfeld on the steps of our apartment building. Sheinfeld is thirty, a sabra, a father of two, a Talmudic scholar, the son of a famous writer, and is known as a highly perceptive young man. He rarely speaks unless spoken to.

"Nu," I said, in search of some comfort and assurance, "what will be with the Egyptians?"

"The Egyptians!" he scoffed. "More of the same. The same old talk, the same old bluff. Surely if Nasser meant business he wouldn't so publicize his troop movements. He's trying to impress the rest of the Arabs. He has no prestige among them, so he's trying to show how tough he is. Surely he knows we can destroy him at any time."

It sounded reasonable and reassuring, but late that night our neighbor Sarah's husband was called to the telephone. It was the army. He had six hours to report. And the next day, we heard of more men called up.

This is a very swift mobilization. Gradually the streets are emptying and all you see are young children, women, older men — and Americans like me who would like to do something but don't know quite what.

9 Iyar

Friday, May 19

OUR YEAR IN ISRAEL is ending not with a whimper but a bang. Here am I, an American rabbi whose home town considers him a bit too Orthodox, living my sabbatical year in the very citadel of world Orthodoxy, Bnei Brak — where I am considered not Orthodox enough. After all, I do not have a full beard, do not wear a long *kapotte* or a fur hat, or long *peyos* — and, worse still, I am lecturing at a university, albeit a religiously oriented university such as Bar Ilan.

Almost everyone in this town is completely observant — 50,000 strong. Only a few miles north of Tel Aviv, it has its own mayor, its own schools, and its own distinctive way of life. First impression: Torah learning and scholarship is taken for granted. Even the grocer, even the common street cleaner, spouts passages from the Bible and Talmud.

During my first night in town, I went into a grocery to pick up some vegetables. There were practically none to be had.

"Is there a vegetable shortage?" I asked.

The grocer, bearded, and with sizeable *peyos*, patiently explained to me that *Shemittah* — the Biblical Sabbatical year when the fields in the Holy Land must lie fallow — has just come to an end. Bnei Brak Jews, together with Orthodox Jews throughout Israel, will eat only the produce from certain farms which have observed the *Shemittah* regulations. And verbatim he quoted the passage from *Vayikra* (25:3): "Six years shall you sow your field... but the seventh year shall be a Sabbath of rest for the land, you shall neither sow your field, nor prune your vineyard."

"Oh my," I said laughingly. "We came to Israel at the wrong time."

"No, my friend," he said, "you came at the right time. Tell me, in America can you fulfill such a Torah *mitzvah?*"

I did come at the right time. Not only for *mitzvos* but for excitement. That grocer, by the way, was mobilized this morning.

Shabbos approaches, the jewel of the Bnei Brak week. But the eve of Shabbos, all of Friday afternoon, with the jostle and bustle of preparation, and the gradual quiet which descends upon the streets, the slowdown which is tangible and visible — all this is almost as beautiful. For the truth is that you do not really have a Shabbos unless you have an *Erev Shabbos*.

Rabbi Akiva Street goes through various stages on Friday afternoon in preparation for Shabbos. A slow, gradual quietude settles over it as the sun goes down and the strange yellow light of late afternoon begins to envelop the town. Then the scurrying of the men to the *mikveh*, brightly hued towels in hand, for their own pre-Shabbos purification, followed by the men with their children hurrying off to the various shuls. The Mizrachi men, distinguished by their tiny knitted *yarmulkes;* the *shtreimlach,* the black socks, the white socks, the *peyos,* the beards, children, *kapottes* — all going off in every direction, because there is a shul in every direction: Bobover and Klausenberger and Vizhnitzer and Belzer and Sanzer and Lelover — all evoking the towns and villages of Eastern Europe that are no more. Sunset. The streets are still, quiet, everyone is at prayer by now. Later in the evening, after everyone has come home, recited *Kiddush,* eaten the Shabbos meal, sung the Shabbos hymns, tested the children on the week's Torah portion, they go out for a short night-time stroll.

The great delight is Shabbos itself. All vehicular traffic is banned and you can walk peacefully down the middle of the main street which is usually rattling with trucks and cars and thick with the acrid fumes of buses.

On Shabbos morning the main street is still. Everyone is in shul. At mid-afternoon, after the morning *seudah,* Torah learning, and a short nap, thousands pour out into the streets. From a distance they look like a black mass, relieved by the stark white of the shirts and the bright colors of the dresses. Children abound, and baby carriages and strollers. Young boys and girls walk in separate groups, banding together for emotional security as they promenade, excitedly talking, up and down the street. For the men, *shtreimlach* are the norm. They come in different shapes and styles: brown fur, lying flat on the head; others upright like an old stove-pipe hat; some are worn rakishly tilted off the forehead, still others are rigorously straight. The *shtreimlached* men wheel the baby carriages and a cortege of children cavorts in the rear.

And then the beginning of sundown. *Shalosh Seudos zemiros* waft out of the various houses and small shuls. You walk along the street hoping that Shabbos will not end, but it grows dark and inevitably the first bus rumbles toward you, honking its horn, the first car snakes its way through the crowds, the men rush off to *Maariv*, the day is over, the week begins. No wonder we sniff the spice box at the end of Shabbos. We need something to counteract the weakness which overcomes us as the Shabbos departs, something to lift the spirits as we begin to face the ordinary days of the week.

10 Iyar

Motza'ei Shabbos, May 20

T IS BEGINNING TO look very serious. On Friday more reservists were called up. All day long they were moving up and down the street in army trucks, jeeps, motor-scooters, and any type of vehicle they could muster. Many were simply taking buses or taxis to the pickup points, others were hitchhiking.

The climax was reached Friday night. Rechov Akiva was alive with tumult. More cars, army buses, jeeps, postmen delivering telegrams, motor-scooters, noise, knocking on doors, ringing telephones. Men were being picked up all night, and even more on Shabbos morning. In our little shul, a soldier walked in, tapped several men on their shoulders as they prayed, they turned, followed him out, went home, said goodbye to their families and went off with him. By now there was no longer a six-hour notice and the men were lucky to get fifteen minutes.

During davening in shul this morning we were constantly interrupted by the roar of traffic outside. Will I ever forget the sight of the men in *shtreimlach* and long black coats, their *peyos* dangling at their sides, riding off to war in jeeps? Did I say war? A slip of the tongue. A Freudian slip? I hope not.

The crisis was of course the main topic in shul and the main subject of the buzzing conversations on the street corners. Tonight I was rather unworried, but everyone's concern is beginning to make me concerned. Anxiety is contagious.

Some of the stories one hears are rather touching. On Friday night a Bnei Brak neighbor is reciting *Kiddush*. A knock at the door. A child runs from the table to open it. A soldier enters. The whole family knows why he has come. They invite him in, he motions to them to continue the *Kiddush*, they complete it, the father sips the wine and distributes it to the family and to the visiting soldier. The father excuses himself without a word, goes into the next room, takes his kit-bag, reappears, kisses his wife goodbye, blesses his children with the traditional Friday night priestly blessing: "May Hashem bless you and keep you. May Hashem turn His countenance upon you and be gracious unto you. May Hashem turn His countenance unto you and give you peace." Dressed in his Shabbos finery he disappears with the soldier.

The pious Jews of Bnei Brak are not only disciplined soldiers but highly disciplined Jews. So when they are mobilized on the Sabbath they have many questions to ask, and they run to the Rabbi. It is Shabbos, shall we go today? (Yes.) Shall we take our *tefillin* along on Shabbos? (Yes.) May we carry our *tallis*? (Yes.) Even the post office, always closed on Shabbos, was wide open today in order to send telegrams and notices to the reservists.

An American student said today that he wants to join the Israeli army and go fight the Arabs.

"You're not afraid of being killed?"

"No."

"Then why don't you go?"

"I'm afraid I'll lose my American citizenship."

The mobilization continues all day, a quiet, efficient hum of activity. The familiar patter of tens of thousands of shoes — men, women, and children — all promenading in their Shabbos best right in the center of the street — this is all gone. The men are called, they go to an appointed corner, they are picked up by an army bus, they board it: the call-up seems so orderly, so efficient, and is working with clocklike precision. There are no pedestrians on the street, only a few watching from the balconies above. The men are home with their families, waiting. When the knock comes at the door it is almost a relief. For him who hears no knock, another long night of waiting is ahead, another day of wondering why he wasn't called. And of rationalizing to himself and to others why he is still walking the streets.

One of our upstairs neighbors, young and apparently able-bodied, is still unmobilized and going about his normal daily business.

Old Mr. Katzenelenbogen downstairs kids him: "Why haven't they called you yet?" I cringe at the question.

The poor fellow replies, "Well, you see, I drive a food truck. I deliver food to the soldiers in their army camps. I suppose I am what you might call in an essential industry." He laughs nervously and tries not to look the old man in the eye. I am embarrassed for him and I turn away.

The wives whose husbands are mobilized are either worried, or calm, or frantic, or resigned, or jealous of those wives whose husbands are still around. They are, in a word, just like soldiers' wives all over the world. Leah next door mutters imprecations at every man who walks down the street. Her husband is in, and they have two small children, so why is this fellow strutting along when he isn't even married? Where is justice, where is right? And yet she keeps telling us to return to America immediately, that it is foolish to stay.

I feel a kind of guilt as I pass by the house of our neighbor whose husband was taken in the middle of the night. She looks at me from her porch. Is she thinking, *Here is an able-bodied man, why isn't he doing his share?* Or am I just too self-conscious? I try to vindicate myself by remembering that if I had wanted to shirk my responsibilities, I could have left the country at the first sign of trouble. Maybe I should get a sign and carry it around: "I AM AN AMERICAN CITIZEN. I AM NOT ALLOWED TO SERVE IN ANOTHER ARMY. BUT I AM NOT LEAVING. I AM STAYING. SO ARE MY WIFE AND CHILDREN." The lady is still looking at me. She doesn't see my sign. She is not impressed. I don't blame her. It doesn't sound very heroic. Well, is it my fault that Nasser starts trouble? What am I supposed to do? I am only an American. I couldn't serve in the Israel army if I wanted to. But I do feel frustrated at my inability to be of some help somewhere.

This morning in shul, during the reading of the Torah, the congregation buzzes with worried whispers. Their talk makes a curious counterpoint to the portion we are reading, *Vayikra* 25, the first part of which deals with the laws of the Sabbatical year. Israel has just completed its Sabbatical year, and Bnei Brak especially has fulfilled all the prohibitions and proscriptions and restrictions with great care and piety. The Sabbatical laws contain a promise in verse 18: "And you shall fulfill My statutes and keep My laws and you shall do them; and you will dwell on the land in security." And again in verse 19: "... and you will dwell in security on your land." Everyone seems to catch his breath at these passages, and there is a hush as they are read by the *baal korei*. And then the regular prophetic portion for today, *Yirmeyahu* 32: the prophet is commanded to buy a field and a dwelling place in the Holy Land because Israel will soon dwell there in peace.

Is someone playing tricks on us? Today's Torah readings are awesome.

Maariv tonight in shul moved me deeply. When the regular service was concluded the *chazan*, instead of leaving the pulpit, remained in place and announced that we would read together *Tehillim*, chapters 83 and 142. And in a loud, wailing chant he led the congregation in *Tehillim* 83, verse by verse. Again I had the feeling that someone was playing tricks on us:

> O God, be not silent; be not quiet, nor be still, O God. For behold, Your enemies make a tumult, and they who hate You have lifted up their heads. Against Your people they shrewdly take counsel, and they plot against those whom You protect. They have said, "Come and let us cut them off from being a nation, so the name of Israel shall be remembered no more. When they plot in their heart together, against You they make a covenant — the tents of Edom and the Ishmaelites, Moav and Hagrim; Geval and Ammon and Amalek, the Philistines with the inhabitants of Tyre. Even Ashur is joined with them; they have become an arm of the children of Lot, *Selah*. Do unto them as unto Midian; as to Sisera, as to Yavin at the River Kishon.

They were annihilated at Ein Dor; they became as dung for the soil... As a fire that burns up a forest and as a flame that sets the mountains ablaze, so pursue them with Your storm and terrify them with Your whirlwind. Fill their faces with shame, that they may seek Your Name, O Lord. Let them be made ashamed and terrified forever, and they will be humiliated and perish. Then they will know that You, Your Name alone is the Eternal, the Most High over all the earth.

When the congregation finished reading it — how passionately we pray when we are in danger — there was a hush over everyone, and my sons Ilan and Jonathan came up to me and said, "Gosh, Abba, we didn't know it was that serious."

11 Iyar

Sunday, May 21

AS I OBSERVE THE amazing efficiency of this call-up, the normal inefficiency of everyday life in Israel stands out in sharp contrast. Three particular examples come to mind: the laboratory, the post office, and the museum.

THE LABORATORY: In Israel the physicians do not give their own hypodermic injections. When you need one, they give you a prescription blank and send you to a special *machon*, or laboratory, which administers the injections.

Just a week ago Ilan needed an ordinary flu shot. We left the doctor's office and found the *machon* a few blocks away. The nurse informed me that she did not have that particular medication. She sent us to a *beit mirkachat*, a drugstore. They did not have it either. We went to another *beit mirkachat*. They were closed. The sign on the door said that they would open at four P.M. It was now four forty-five. A long line was forming on the sidewalk. We gave up and found a third *beit mirkachat.* They did not have what we needed. We went home. No shot.

THE POST OFFICE: Similar confusion reigns at the post office. I wait in line for ten minutes to send a package. At the head of the line, finally, a clerk tells me quite crankily that for this kind of package I have to go across to the other counter for weighing. I point weakly to the scale that is beside him. He retorts that he is sorry but he cannot weigh it here; it must be weighed across the aisle. I dutifully go to the other counter, and wait in line again. When my turn comes, the clerk is irritated: "The man over there is wrong. He is the one who is supposed to weigh it. But anyway, give it to me and I will weigh it for you." I ask him how many stamps it will need. He does not know. For this, he says, I will have to go back to the first counter. He can only tell me how much it weighs, but the clerk at the first counter will determine how many stamps I will need. I return to the first line again. I have spent forty-five minutes. I try to smile.

THE MUSEUM: Last month the family and I made a special trip to the famous Glass Museum north of Tel Aviv, which, according to its own brochure and its advertisements, is open daily until five. We arrived at three. The curator was closing up.

"But your own sign says that you are open until five," I protested.

"I'm the only one in charge here, and I don't have the patience to stay open until five. I know the papers and the brochure say five, but I'm alone here and I have no help and so I am closing up. I close up every day at three."

"So why don't you at least change your brochure and your ads so that people like us will not make special trips for nothing?"

"That is not my business. If the authorities want to change the time they can do it. Officially it *is* open until five; I am just closing it unofficially at three."

"Well then, maybe you can let us see the museum unofficially."

He did not like my joke. "I am sorry, it is three o'clock and I am closing up."

If one keeps his sense of humor all this can be rather amusing. But in critical times this kind of *meshugaas* can be tragic. And this is just the point. In view of the pathetic bumbling, hopeless red-tape, and buck-passing bureaucracy of almost every aspect of public and governmental life in Israel, the remarkable efficiency of the mobilization is miraculous.

The call-up was almost completed in forty-eight hours. Anyone who was not at home when the call came found a red-lettered notice on his door giving detailed instructions about where and when to report. Every man keeps a special bag in his closet just for such occasions. And every so often they have dress rehearsals: the army runs an occasional surprise mobilization drill to keep the machinery well-oiled. The men gripe at these drills — which come at odd hours of the day or night — but the last few days show how important they are. Some 80,000 men have gone from their homes and businesses to their battle stations — all in a matter-of-fact, business-like manner, without great show of emotion or fanfare. Some units have reported 110% call-up. One thing is clear: there are no draft-card burners in Israel. They have something close and real and tangible to fight for, and their morale is high.

12 Iyar

Monday, May 22

A S I DRIVE INTO Bar Ilan University today, three army buses are loading up students in the campus parking lot. Many of these boys are trained parachutists, some of my students among them. Suddenly the mobilization is no longer a cold, objective fact which I can observe and chronicle with detachment. The sight of these smiling young students — eighteen-, nineteen-, twenty-year-olds — duffle bags in hand, climbing into the buses, hits me in the pit of my stomach. My students. Off to war. To be killed, to be maimed, to suffer heat and cold and starvation. My students, my boys. I had not realized that I had grown attached enough to them to become maudlin or sentimental. All the tensions and fears of the past week well up within me, and I sit in the car in silence, watch them load up, and weep. It is such a bright, crisp, blue morning.

They might be going off to a football game, so carefree

do they seem. I want to rush over to them, embrace each one, kiss them goodbye, wish them good fortune. But I cannot spoil their mood, even if it is only a front for fear, and so I sit alone in the car and watch them drive off. May the God of Israel be with them.

In the class that follows, only female students are present. The boys have almost all been mobilized, and those few who have not been called are ashamed to come to class.

I wonder to myself how Rachamim is getting along. Rachamim, a Yemenite boy, has not been at a lecture for two weeks. He had had difficulty with some facial muscles. Nothing serious, but the doctor has prescribed complete bed rest. Rachamim — the name, meaning mercy, enthralls me — is a poor student. A lightly built eighteen-year-old with a ready smile and a bright wit, he is charming and pleasant, darkly handsome, very popular, and very lazy.

I have told him he is going to fail. Rachamim is convinced, how-ever, that I will not fail him, and in order to support his conviction he has of late embarked on a campaign of flattery.

"Rachamim," I say, "you are going to fail."

"You are the finest lecturer in the university. We will not let you go back to America. You must stay here with us in Israel."

"Rachamim, you are going to fail because you do not do any work at all."

"Yes, we are getting up a petition to keep you here. America can live without you. We cannot live without you."

"Rachamim, you are going to fail because you are nothing but a flatterer. That is the only thing you do well in this class."

"We already have three hundred names on the petition. Even the faculty is signing it. We will make you president of the univer-sity." His huge black eyes are fixed upon me as he speaks. I really think he believes what he is saying at the moment.

I feel somehow a kinship with Rachamim — and it is not only the unabashed and uninhibited way in which he flatters — and I miss him. I ask one of the girls if she knows how he's feeling.

"Oh, Rachamim? He was called up two nights ago."

"But he is sick. He is confined to bed. Doctor's orders."

"When they came for him he told them he wanted to go but he must speak to his doctor first. They said they had no time, and he could speak to the Air Force doctor."

"Air Force doctor?"

"Yes, Rachamim is a paratrooper."

"Rachamim?"

I wonder if Rachamim flattered his way into the paratroopers. With his talents, he should be chief of staff before the crisis is over. I will miss him. My ego will miss him. But I will still have to fail him. *Rachamim*, O God, on Rachamim and on all of us.

13 Iyar

Tuesday, May 23

AFTER *SHACHARIS* AT SHUL my friend Bonner comes up to me. (I call him my friend Bonner because of that day two months ago when I suddenly got two flat tires during a driving rainstorm. I was totally helpless, since in Israel there is no such thing as calling up a gas station to help with tires — especially in the rain. They simply tell you to bring the tire to a "specialist." How do you get the tire to a specialist when it's flat and when you can't change it yourself? They are very polite, but they don't quite know how this can be managed. They simply encourage you and tell you to try. Suddenly Bonner appeared in his truck on his way to work, saw my predicament, and spent over two hours with me helping me change the tires, bringing them in for repairs, and generally amazing me and touching me deeply with his genuine consideration and kindness. Up until that morning we had been only casual acquaintances who occasionally would nod to each other in shul, with that reserve and detachment which marks the relationship of Israelis with the "Anglo-Saxonim," as they call us.)

He taps me on the shoulder.

"Did you hear the news?" he says with a faint smile.

"What news?"

"Nasser has closed the Straits of Tiran. He says if Israel wants war he is now more than ready and willing."

I am stunned. "Are you sure, or is it just a rumor?" There are so many rumors these days that one has to verify and evaluate everything he hears.

"I am sure," he says. This time the smile is gone. "Don't worry, it's not a rumor." (Don't worry!)

"Where did you hear it?"

"This morning on the six o'clock news."

"Is it official, or just a radio rumor?"

Now he is smiling again. "No, no, it's official. He closed the Straits of Tiran. He claims they belong to him."

"But that's a declaration of war."

"Yes, exactly. So maybe now you'll leave."

"I'll see."

"You really ought to leave. There's no point in staying. You have a wife, you have children, you're scheduled to leave in any case in two weeks. So leave now. If I could, I would leave, too."

I resort to my stock answer: "You know I can't leave you here by yourself to fight the Arabs."

"No," he says, "be serious. I am interested to know why you are staying. It intrigues me."

"I am not sure," I say. "It's because of many things. One of them is that we are not really afraid — so far. We think everything will turn out all right."

This seems to satisfy him, and he repeats my words. "You think everything will turn out all right. Good, good. Now at least I hear a reason. I hope you're right. By the way, what about the American government? Haven't they told you to get out?"

"Yes, they have."

"*That's* a government for you. Worries about its citizens, tries always to protect them. America — what a country!"

As I leave shul I am less moved by America's concern for me than I am by the crisis itself. I walk home. The streets seem emptier every day. Even the buses are running less frequently, since almost all the drivers have been mobilized. One thing is clear: our decision to stay or leave has to be made, and made quickly. But it is obviously not easy. For example, my American friend Harry made up his mind the other day to send his four children back to the United States. He purchased tickets, made reservations, and his children came over to say goodbye to us. But that same evening I met them on the street.

"What happened?"

Sheepishly, they answered, "Daddy changed his mind. He says there'll be no war."

Well, if Daddy says so...

This morning as I walk home from shul I run into Harry. He smiles when he sees me, but he is worried.

"Come on," he says, "tell me something pleasant. Some good news. Please."

I know that he is not simply joking. Things look so bleak and one feels so trapped and surrounded that any kind of rumor — even if we know it is false — is pleasant as long as it is a good rumor. I haven't heard any good false rumors lately — only bad true rumors — nor do I have the heart to tell him about Nasser and the Straits so early in the morning, so I just stand there and grin foolishly.

"Come on, tell me something. Anything."

"Anything?"

"Anything," he laughs. "Anything at all."

So I tell him. The Straits of Tiran are blockaded.

"Come on, come on, Manny, you must be kidding. That's ridiculous. He wouldn't dare."

"Well, Bonner told me in shul. I hope he's wrong, but he's usually right. He says he heard it on the six o'clock news."

"*Gottenyu!*" He exclaims. "Maybe the news broadcast made a mistake. You never know these days."

"True. It could be an error. Let's hope so."

But it is no error, and as the day rolls along it becomes perfectly clear that the noose is tightening around our necks. Nasser's sudden arrogance and bravado are obviously due to Russian backing. He stood quietly by during the Samua raid in November and during the downing of six Migs in Syria last month. Now he can reassert himself as the tough and faithful leader of the Arabs.

I meet Bura on the street at seven A.M., just after *Shacharis*. He is smiling as always: seven A.M., seven P.M., it doesn't matter. What a genial, happy person. Twenty-eight years old, married, a number of children, he wears a full beard, long *peyos*, and, on Shabbos, a long black silken *kapotte*. Every morning at seven sharp he walks up the street, his two little girls in tow, on the way to nursery school and kindergarten. He always looks a bit sheepish with one child in each hand, but he obviously likes doing it while his wife is busy at home with the three younger ones, ages three, two, and six months. Bura is smart, native-born, and knows politics and Israel thoroughly. His father is a bank president in Tel Aviv and walks in the councils of the mighty, which makes Bura privy to certain intelligence reports about what is or might be going on. In the past his information and theories, if not always perfectly accurate, have at least had the distinction of being logical, which has not always been the case with most of the theories one hears around here.

He shakes my hand warmly when he sees me. "You are not leaving?"

I am getting bored with the question. "No," I reply vaguely.

"Why not?" He likes to analyze and now he is analyzing me. His eyes narrow imperceptibly.

"I don't know."

"Many other Americans are leaving, you know." He is baiting me.

"Yes, I know. But meanwhile we are here. After all, do you think I want to leave you over here all by yourself to fight the Arabs?"

The reply is growing stale with me. I shall have to develop a new one. Perhaps it would help if I were to find out why we are really staying. This still puzzles me.

He presses on. "Listen, all jokes aside, it really is silly to leave. Let's look at it rationally. What might be the worst that could happen? There will be a war, right? Well, if there's a war, the fighting will not take place in our town but far away in the desert. And what's the worst thing that might happen in a war? Bombing and shelling? There will be no bombing and shelling, this is certain. In the Sinai Campaign there was one solitary air-raid alert, and that was all. So why leave the country?"

I don't bother to remind him that "far away in the desert" is all of forty miles. After all, to him it's not forty miles but almost one hundred kilometers, which by Israeli standards, is worlds away. But he does sound as if he knows a great deal, and his eyes are wise and convincing. And it feels nice, I must admit, to be reassured.

I do not teach today and on the spur of the moment we decide to pack into the car and drive up to Jerusalem and do some touring. We assume that it won't be too crowded today, and we are right. The roads are absolutely still. The only traffic is the army convoys moving in every direction and an occasional ambassador's car speeding from Jerusalem towards Tel Aviv.

We visit the Knesset. It is a good experience. None of the Knesset members seem unduly alarmed. They are dozing away, as usual, during the speeches. Mrs. Shulamit Aloni, whom I met last year in the States and who subsequently got herself elected to the Knesset, has not changed at all. She is in a bright red and blue sleeveless dress, her hair a mop of dyed orange. A few seats away from her sits the Druze delegate in his Arab headdress and his flowing black and white robes. Directly across the aisle sit the Agudath Israel delegates representing the Orthodox Jews, Rabbis Levine and Lorincz, with long beards and curled *peyos*. All the Knesset members are reading their favorite newspapers while the speeches drone on. Somehow, it is all very comforting and reassuring.

How beautiful and spiritual is Jerusalem: the graceful rolling hills, the ever-changing colors, the blue and pink and orange sunsets, the chilly evenings even in midsummer, the strange, yellow light of the afternoons, and most of all, the emotional and deeply religious associations which the name Jerusalem evokes.

We have been in Jerusalem many times this year.

How easily that slides off the tongue. In any language. Hebrew:

Hayinu biYerushalayim kama p'amim; Yiddish: *Mir zeinin geven in Yerushalayim fieleh mahl.* A few words. A few miles. A few minutes to get there. If you live in Israel (more words that slide trippingly off the tongue) you can get there by bus or train. Or by car if you own one. If you live abroad, you can get there in style by jet (eleven hours from New York, six hours from London) or by ship (two weeks).

But this is too glib, too easy. This is not true. I am imagining.

In 1840 a man set out from Poland to Jerusalem to see the Holy City before he died. He left just after Succos. He arrived in Palestine, spent, sick, exhausted, in time for Pesach eighteen months later. He had crossed mountains and rivers and had fought off marauders and disease. There were many such men in the nineteenth century.

In 1740 a man set out from Russia for Jerusalem to see the Holy City before he died. He bade his wife and children a tearful goodbye, for he knew full well that he might never see them again. Twenty-five months later he set foot on holy soil. But he never got to Jerusalem. Weak and diseased from his travels, he died as he was making his way up the Judean hills which surround the city. He was buried in holy soil. There were many such men in the eighteenth century, and in all the previous centuries as well.

We were in Jerusalem during Pesach. We have been in Jerusalem several times this year.

But this is too glib, too easy. This is not true. I am imagining.

It has been a long day, the children are getting tired, and we turn back towards Tel Aviv. Just on the outskirts of Jerusalem I drive into a filling station, and as the attendant checks the oil, I ask him idly how things are going. He begins suddenly to sob. His son, father of three, has just been called up, is somewhere in the desert, his wife is expecting a fourth.

"I am worried," he says. "What will be, what will be?"

Lamely and ineptly I pat him on the back and assure him that all will be well.

The radio has been announcing for the past two days that there are enough supplies of food to last three full months, and that therefore there is no need to hoard. This only triggers more hoarding. The cupidity of people emerges in a time of crisis, and also their generosity and goodness. Sarah calls down to us from her balcony: "I have plenty of sugar. If you need, just ask." But the five-year-old girl in the apartment below us tells us in wide-eyed innocence that her mother says there's going to be a long war but that they need not worry because they have one bureau drawer full of sugar, another with matzos, and a suitcase full of salt. What will she do with all that salt, war or no war? Later in the day, Estelle goes out on the porch to hang out some wash, and there on the porch below us she sees cases of garlic. Garlic? Even if the poor lady finds some use for the salt, what will she do with all that garlic? I suppose, though, that I shouldn't be too hard on her. After all, she is a survivor of the German concentration camps, and she knows what it is to go hungry. Can one blame her for trying to avoid it? We have refused to hoard so far, but this type of thing is contagious and makes us feel rather foolish. Perhaps we should begin storing up a few things here and there.

I see my brother Aharon in the evening — he has been living here for seven years — and I complain to him about the hoarding, and how I think that it is immoral and that it is actually like stealing from others. He scoffs and tells me not to be a boy scout. He agrees that it is wrong, he himself has not hoarded, but what do I want from people who have known hunger and starvation in Europe?

"Not all these hoarders," I reply, "have known hunger and starvation in Europe. Many of the hoarders are local-born."

Replies Aharon: "Then they've heard it from their parents, all of whom were familiar with it."

I argue that it is still morally wrong and that Jews should know better.

"Come off it," he retorts. "Don't be so high and mighty. Do you think you're giving a sermon now? These people are only doing the natural thing, and you'd do the same thing if you were in their position. It's only because you've been lucky enough never to go hungry in your life that you can have such equanimity right now."

14 Iyar

Wednesday, May 24

IN SHUL THIS MORNING one of the older men figured out that the numerical equivalent of U Thant is the numerical equivalent of Bilam ben Beor: 472. Bilam wanted to destroy the Jews; U Thant wants to destroy the Jews. U Thant will come to the same end as Bilam. It is obvious that U Thant is not the most popular man in Israel at the moment.

The children returned from their daily grocery store visit this morning empty handed: No bread, no eggs, no sugar. People are still hoarding.

Rumors fly and soon become fact. Today I heard this one: the U.S. Marines may land in Haifa. I also heard that the American Sixth Fleet is already in Haifa.

How do you know?

I saw them from the top of the Shalom Tower in Tel Aviv (the tallest building in Israel).

How do you know it was the Sixth Fleet you saw? After all, that's fifty miles away from the Shalom Tower.

Well, they certainly look like American ships.

Oh, that's not true what you say, says another. I saw the Sixth Fleet at Ashdod.

How do *you* know?

Well, I didn't actually see them, but my upstairs neighbor told me that he heard about it, and it must be true. Johnson won't let the Egyptians do anything to us so he'll surely send the Sixth Fleet to Ashdod.

Interesting how shared danger makes friends of everyone. I stop at a light in the middle of cold, impersonal Tel Aviv, and a driver pulls up alongside, leans out his window and says to me, "*Yihyeh tov* — All will be good." There are so many "*Yihyeh tov*"s that methinks the country protests too much. Everyone is trying to assure himself by assuring his neighbor. And the interesting thing about it all is that it does help.

But there is deep tension in the air. How long can those two huge armies in the desert face each other without fighting? And meanwhile, Israel's economy is suffering, with so many people at the front and nobody home to watch the store — literally.

Our neighbor Leah, a young mother of two, said to me today in genuine surprise, "You haven't gone yet? Why not?"

I give her answer number two: "And leave you here to fight the Arabs all by yourself?"

She looks me squarely in the eye, shrugs her shoulders, and says, "If I had the chance, I'd leave."

Her remark stuns me. One thing about these Israelis: they do not pose. No mock heroics for them.

Yesterday's news that Jordan is allowing Iraqi troops into her borders is another turn of the screw. The enemies of Israel, even though they may despise each other, somehow manage to unite when it comes to hating Israel. And the subsequent news that the Security Council is adjourning without setting a new date for another meeting is a further tightening. Gloom settles over Israel like a fog. U.S. denial that she ever threatened to use force against Nasser helps make things worse. It is gradually dawning on all of us, this age-old agonizing truth: no one in the world really cares about Israel. Any illusions we might have had about the unquestioning friendship of the United States or of France are now shattered. France says she is neutral, obviously trying to court the Arabs. And this from the great moralizer himself, DeGaulle. How have the mighty fallen! The world visionary, the epitome of integrity and statesmanship, Le Grand Charles turns out to be as phony as the rest. This is only the beginning of the end for him, I am convinced. As soon as they tamper with the Jews they are starting on their way down. Chauvinism? Nationalistic pride? No. Like it or not, the Jews are a holy people and those who touch it in the wrong manner must inevitably become burned.

Is the U.S. much better? She makes pretty speeches and issues platitudes. And England — lovable England, which runs a close second only to the Germans in the affection of the Israelis — England is sending its well-groomed diplomats with their carefully trimmed mustaches all over the world in an effort to look important.

See my diplomat.

Watch him fly.

THE 28TH OF IYAR

Here he is.

There he goes.

See his nice clothes.

Hear him speak.

Let's face it: Despite all the protestations about territorial integrity and the rights of nations and freedom of navigation, it does seem, doesn't it, that the free world is going to be quite content to sit idly by and fold its hands and allow another two and a half million Jews to be slaughtered. *Al tivtechu binedivim*, do not trust in princes. And the Catholic Church? They who are now so ecumenical, so repentant about what they have done to the Jews over the years, so forgiving, so embarrassed over their silence during World War II — what are they saying now? An ominous, deathly silence thunders forth from the Vatican.

15 Iyar

Thursday, May 25

TODAY'S NEWS IS LUDICROUS: Iraq announces that she is not sending troops to Jordan because Jordan "waited too long before agreeing to allow us in." My English translation from the Arabic: Jordan refuses them entry, period, because Jordan distrusts Iraq. The announcement was greeted with laughter by the Israelis: "*Aravim!* Arabs!" they all jeered.

That which was a shock yesterday and seemed too tense to bear is today bearable and acceptable as if we were always living with it. Tiran blocked? On Monday it would have seemed impossible to live with. Today it is part of life. Tiran mined? On Tuesday it would have been inconceivable. Today it is normal.

Nothing has changed, yet today people somehow are a bit less grim than yesterday. Stores had been empty of goods, but are reportedly normal today. We have been able to get bread and a few other necessities without too much waiting in line. Behind the change of mood, of course, is the fact that humans simply like to be optimists.

You wonder about this optimism, this human heart in which hope springs eternal. My God! In the Warsaw Ghetto, the diarists write that even at the end few of the people believed that they were going to be slaughtered. Roosevelt wouldn't allow it, Churchill wouldn't permit it, Hitler wouldn't dare, etc., etc. And always there were theorists who were able to find a silver lining. The similarity with today is frightening. More than frightening: ghastly. Are we fooling ourselves, and closing our eyes to reality the way they did? It is too terrible a thought to go to sleep on, but my eyes are closing on me, and I must sleep.

We are still being good American boy scouts and are not hoarding, but I do keep the car's gas tank filled at all times. If this crisis keeps up there is bound to be gas rationing. I resist the temptation, however, to fill up an extra can of gasoline. Not after all my moralizing about hoarding.

In the early afternoon my brother Aharon comes over. He hates to impose, but I must drive him into Tel Aviv to the American Embassy to arrange for his family's passports in case Americans are evacuated. No buses are running, no taxicabs. I reluctantly agree, muttering something about nobody's going to evacuate because it won't be necessary.

"Why are you so reluctant to take me down there? This is an emergency. I have a wife and six children, you have a wife and four children. I can't understand how you can be so calm in such an emergency. You are out of your mind."

(Neither can I understand why I am not more nervous.)

We drive into Tel Aviv. The streets are empty. The usual twenty minute ride takes half the time. I never thought a lack of traffic would depress me.

The Embassy is crowded. There are lines around the block, Americans trying to get out. Eight thousand have left in two days. TWA and the other airlines have sent in special planes. You have to know someone to get a ticket. All the travel agencies are packed, and Air France, Alitalia, Swissair — all the airlines on Hayarkon Street near the Embassy — have long lines of people clamoring for seats.

In front of the Embassy I meet a young American. "Where are you going?" I ask.

"Switzerland. That's the only place I can get a flight to. From there I'll see. But I'm getting out. Tonight."

Schwarzman, an American neighbor of ours, comes out of the Embassy. "I'm leaving tonight," he says rather breathlessly.

"Oh," I say. "Good luck." I can see he is not too happy about it and I try to ease the pain.

"I don't know if I'm doing the right thing," he says. "I hear the Sixth Fleet is coming. Maybe everything will be O.K. Do you think I should stay?"

"Look," I say, "the Sixth Fleet isn't going to do anything. Don't base any decisions on them."

"Anyway I was leaving in July," he says a little nervously, "so I'll leave now. My wife is expecting and she can't take the tension. We didn't even pack. I hope we're making the right decision."

"It will be all right. Don't worry."

What else can I say? I feel sorry for him, but it is disquieting to hear that he is leaving with his family. Sanders left last week with his wife and six children, Reuven is sending his wife and children to Italy. The wave of panic spreads. And flights are all booked.

There is no question that the Israelis deeply resent Americans who leave the country after having lived here for years. No one blames American tourists for leaving, but when American residents pull out after having settled here, all the old and deeply-rooted antagonisms come to the surface:

"Americans!" they sniff. "Soft and fat. Babies!"

"First sign of trouble, and it's back to the Motherland."

"Who needs them?"

"And this we called settling in the Holy Land!"

"They ought not to allow them ever to come back."

A further tightening of the screw. Nasser says the Straits are not only blockaded but mined against Israeli shipping. The question of the hour: how does the mine know if it is about to blow up an Israeli ship or an Arab ship? Answer: since it is Egyptian, it is a mine of anti-Jewishness.

Today I received a wire from some friends in Atlanta. It read: WE ARE CONCERNED FOR YOU AND YOUR FAMILY. SUGGEST YOU TAKE NEXT PLANE OUT. DON'T BE A HERO. I wire back immediately: WHO'S A HERO? SEE *VAYIKRA* 26:6. (That happens to be this week's Torah portion.)

In Tel Aviv to buy some books, I stop at an oceanfront cafe for a drink. It is a beautiful, warm afternoon, the sky is that special Mediterranean blue, and the sea has hardly a ripple, only an occasional lapping wave here and there. Just south of us, down in the desert, several hundred thousand men are sweating it out —

literally and figuratively — in their scorching tanks. A few men are huddled around the cafe radio, listening to the ubiquitous news.

Israelis are constant — and hopelessly indiscriminate — radio addicts. How ludicrous: in Bnei Brak, whenever I walk by the apartment of one of the great local scholars, his wife is working to the voice of Perry Como's "Some Enchanted Evening." She does not know what the words mean, and this is fortunate. The normal radio fare here is rather poor: 1950s vintage American music, the type that does not grow better with age. I dread the thought of TV when it comes to Israel. But there are compensations: live symphony concerts are broadcast regularly, as well as an occasional stimulating talk program. And now, thanks to the crisis, we have news programs every hour, instead of the customary four times a day.

I am beginning to admire these newscasters. They can make every broadcast sound as if they are presenting significant developments, when upon reflection you discover that nothing has transpired that you didn't know before. But it is comforting nevertheless to hear the steady, almost reassuring voice of the announcer. This fellow Emek Peri of Kol Yisrael Radio is almost like a friend of the family. We love him. He soothes, comforts, calms, reassures, and restores our soul, all by the matter-of-fact manner in which he reads the news. He doesn't have the class of a Huntley or the wit of a Brinkley or the erudition of a Cronkite or the depth of a Sevareid — he is probably only a hack who reads what others have prepared for him — but he is all we have and we love him. All the announcers at Kol Yisrael are excellent, with voices well-modulated and words clearly enunciated, but Peri is our boy.

Listening to the news, by the way, has of late become an art form in its own right. One has to time his every move so that he will be at a radio for the hourly broadcast. And if you carry a transistor radio with you, you are mobbed every hour on the hour. People clamor to get near you, they cup their ears to listen, they jostle each other to get closer, and amid the tumult you manage to glean the essence of the news: Johnson reaffirms *sha!*, Harold Wilson regrets *sheket!*, DeGaulle hopes *ooh!*, Nasser threatens *feh!*, the Israeli Cabinet declares *ah!*, Moscow states *oy!*, Cairo warns *sheket!* Nothing is new.

I muse about all this during the news broadcast in the cafe, and as a result hear nothing.

"Any news?" I ask.

They turn to me. One of them says good-naturedly, "Bah! Your Johnson. What good is he? Words, words, only words he gives us. What we need are arms, weapons. If Johnson is a man, he sends us a few dozen bombers, some fighters, tanks."

"Who needs Johnson?" says another. "We have enough planes and tanks — and we have good soldiers. With our tanks we can clobber Nasser today."

Always sermonizing, I butt in: "With our tanks, and with our God."

"Our God," he sighs. "Where was our God in Europe? Where was our God during the Holocaust? No, we need bullets and tanks, not our God."

"You are wrong," I say.

The news listeners gather around us, waiting for a good argument.

He says, "You are an American and you are taking up for God? In America they still believe in God?"

"Not only in America. Even in Israel. Even you believe in God."

"I believe, I do not believe, what does it matter? Right now only tanks matter. Tanks and planes. The soldiers we have, thank God."

54

The "thank God" trips off his tongue so naturally that he is not even aware of it.

"You live in Israel," I say. "How many generations before Jews have lived on their own Jewish soil? You are the first in two thousand years. Doesn't this mean something to you?"

"Of course, but what do you mean?"

"I mean that we are fully ready to accept God's miracle in giving us a land — this we say we do understand. For two thousand years we have had nothing; now suddenly we have something. And this is for us no problem. This is for us logical. And yet isn't this just as mysterious and beyond understanding as the Holocaust? Especially since they both happened almost at the same time?"

The little knot of people wait for his reply. Suddenly he smiles and takes my arm. "I don't know," he says. "I don't know. Maybe you are right. But God knows we need tanks."

Everyone laughs.

I must record once again the emptiness of Tel Aviv. This bustling, vivacious city, always crowded and on the move, is almost completely barren of young men. One sees only women, children, elderly men — and foreigners like me. *How does she sit solitary, the city that was full of people is become like a widow.*

This is a country that is girding for war. One gets the feeling of living inside a coiled spring, with only a slight touch needed to set it off. Nobody here wants a war, but almost everyone is accepting that possibility with a kind of stoic resignation. As Bura said the other day at the famous Itchkovitch *shtiebelach*, "This is the price a Jew has to pay to stay alive. In Russia, it was the pogrom. It used to come like clockwork. And here in Israel, it's the regular war. Also like clockwork." True enough. But at least here the Jew can defend himself. That is, he can defend himself at the front. I don't know how cities like Tel Aviv or Haifa or Jerusalem are going to defend themselves from air attack or missile bombardment.

Sad to think of all this in this glorious springtime: the wild-flowers, bright iridescent red and gold and yellow and pink and or-ange and blue, the sun warm and soothing. You try to hide it and cover up and hope that things will work out, but for some reason, those wild flowers create an even deeper despair.

Like a thermometer the national temperature rises or falls, the mood is optimistic or pessimistic, depending on the latest news broadcast. We listen hungrily to the radio, and our hopes and fears go up, down, up, down, with every report. When George Brown says something hopeful, everyone smiles; when Lyndon Johnson says something non-committal, everyone droops; when Harold Wilson says there must be freedom of the seas, we are happy; when DeGaulle refuses to say anything, we begin to worry all over again. We tune in to the BBC and Voice of America to get their views, and all we hear is gobbledygook in English. The new Esperanto: gobble-dygook. In Hebrew, in English, it means the same.

The big question now is whether or not Israel will run the block-ade. BBC thinks that Israel will wait for the support of the maritime powers and will not do anything unilaterally. Voice of America pres-ents news analysts who flail away at the air. Kol Yisrael Radio is mum, since it is government-controlled, and no one wants to give any hints about Israel's next move. Only on the streets of Bnei Brak and on the other streets of Israel does everyone know exactly what Israel's next move will be. Each citizen is certain that he and he alone knows the real facts.

But this must be said: if a vote were taken in Israel's streets tonight, running the blockade singlehandedly would win by a landslide. The people are simply not in a mood for a waiting game. They want to get it over with. They — we — are impatient and angry with all the dilly-dallying and cabinet meetings and statements. We are isolated, surrounded, and we know full well that the outside world cares nothing at all about us. What is that old Hebrew expression? *V'al mah yesh lanu l'hishaen, al Avinu she'baShamayim:* We can depend on no one except our Father in heaven.

But can the Israeli man in the street be patient enough to wait if need be, or will he clamor for action and force the government to fight before it is ready? The Israeli is so fiery, so impatient, so impulsive: I wonder if he has the strength to sweat out more than a week or two of this. More than anything else this is a test of nerve. The strain shows on everyone's face.

We say our *Avinu Malkeinu* fervently every morning and evening, and we recite *Tehillim* 83 and 142 — and we wait. The passion with which these prayers are recited should be enough to make a breakthrough into the councils of the Almighty. As I read these *Tehillim* the thought occurs to me that God certainly will not allow another two and one-half million Jews in Israel to be slaughtered. Not after Europe. Not a mere twenty-five years later. But who am I to speak for God? One thing is certain: Rarely in our history have so many Jews prayed so ardently. Will anyone laugh when I say that this is our secret weapon?

On the subject of secret weapons, an interesting bit of information came to light outside of Itchkovitch tonight. As always, the sidewalk and street were glutted with small knots of people in animated discussion. But Schwab had attracted the biggest crowd. (It was between *Minchah* and *Maariv* and almost everyone in Bnei Brak was there.)

Schwab is a prosperous, middle-aged real estate man, tall, thin, deeply suntanned, very handsome in his grey goatee, always riding about on an old bicycle. He used to smuggle arms to the Haganah on a bicycle during the British occupation. Probably the same bike.

Schwab was saying tonight that we have a secret weapon. One of his best friends, an army officer, told him about it. If true, it's fantastic. It's a kind of missile that is buried underground and which fires not one but dozens of missiles simultaneously. Each missile is magnetic and is attracted to heat or to metal. Schwab's eyes gleamed as he described the weapon.

I met Mrs. Katzenelenbogen sweeping the sidewalk in front of the apartment today. I said to her, "Oh, if you're sweeping, all will be well."

"They put us in a filthy ghetto in Europe, and I swept there, too."

"*Yihyeh tov*," I say lamely.

"What do they want from us? Wherever we are, they persecute us. In Europe I lost my sisters, my brothers. I'm the only one left. Why don't they let us be?"

I decide today to try to do something concrete, instead of merely going through the motions of daily existence. There are no more classes to speak of, all the students have evaporated, and I simply must do something to help out in some way. I drive into Tel Aviv and try to find the army mobilization headquarters, which is no easy task. But when I finally discover it, after hours of wandering back and forth through the central city, it is worth all the effort. The citizens may be tense and worried, but the soldiers are quite relaxed. They are joking, drinking soda, and a pushcart peddler is doing a roaring business selling falafel and orange juice. I approach a small group of young soldiers and tell them I want to offer myself and my car to drive soldiers or people wherever they need to go. Their reaction is one of sheer amazement, shock, gratitude.

"But you are an American, are you not?"

"Yes, but I would like to help in some way."

They are delighted. Four of them fairly pick me up and sweep me into the commanding officer's room.

"He is an American, and he wants to help out," they all say to him excitedly.

The commanding officer, very, very British with his mustache and his mien, is also very pleased. "Let me take your name and address, and we will be in touch with you as soon as we need you. There may be another call-up this evening and if so we will have to have your car to help us out. We appreciate it."

On the way back to my car one of the soldiers, about eighteen years old, says to me: "We have a tiny napkin for a country. It's just a speck on the map. But if they don't let us be, we'll give it to Nasser over the head again — and this time it will be for keeps."

As I climb into the car and drive away, I overhear the soldiers calling out to a passing officer, "That was an American. He wants to help us out."

I must record in some way the lump in my throat as I watched our little Chavah this morning rounding the corner, oblivious to everyone, gaily traipsing off to school, bag of books at her side, lunch in her arm, braids jangling, completely unconcerned with the tensions and pressures and impending bloodshed. She is bouncing off to school, she is crossing a street by herself, she will hear a story from her teacher, she has on a bright new dress, she is six years old, and mommy has fixed her braids: what else matters?

16 Iyar

Friday, May 26

T HE SMALLER THE TOWN, the greater the tension seems to be, the more visible the emptiness of the streets, the more palpable and tangible the absence of the men. Even Tel Aviv is ghost-like, without traffic, without people, like a city in a trance. But the Mediterranean that suddenly surprises you at the end of Allenby Street is just as blue and calm and pretty, beautiful, peaceful, soft, inviting (what adjectives shall one use?) as it has always been. After all, the Mediterranean has been around for a long time, has seen crises and wars and turmoil, and I suppose it just isn't impressed by these things anymore. Which is the kind of pathetic fallacy a writer is not supposed to use, but this is war.

Posters have appeared on every shul wall and on every storefront in Bnei Brak. They are signed by all the rabbis of the city and they call on all the citizens to have faith in

61

God, for all will surely be well, and they remind one and all that it is our duty to do *teshuvah*, to return to God and to His Torah, and especially to perform the *mitzvos* with greater fervor and intention.

A new rumor and everyone is overjoyed: Johnson has threatened Nasser with force. He has sent a secret message to him and informed him that unless the Straits of Tiran are opened immediately, the United States will force them open. The rumor is patently false, but why not enjoy it while it lasts?

One of the interesting side conversations you overhear concerns the various Chassidic Rebbeim and their opinions about the crisis. Of course, much of this is also hearsay and theory and rumor. For example, it is now said that the Vizhnitzer Rebbe has said that Nasser will begin to fall this weekend. The American Chassidim who are stranded in Israel are scurrying to their various Rebbeim to ask their advice about staying or leaving. The Lubavitcher Rebbe is said to have instructed his Chassidim to remain in Israel, as has the Gerrer Rebbe. Even the Satmar Rebbe, who will recognize only a messianic state in Israel, has reportedly predicted a major triumph for the "Zionists."

But if the Chassidim are staying, there are more "Anglosaxonim" leaving every hour. Each of them has his own apology, his own excuse, his own rationalization. They need not really feel so guilty. They are doing only what is natural and should not be condemned. But they are missing the exhilaration of being part of all of this. *Al tifrosh min ha-tzibur*, says Hillel in the Mishnah,

Do not separate yourself from the community.

The passages in davening keep coming alive as if I were seeing them for the first time, such as the line in *Birkas Hamazon*: "And may food never be lacking for us forever and ever..." Or the first few passages of this week's Torah reading, referring to Israel's living on the land in security. And last week's as well: "And you shall dwell on the land in safety." And the remarkable interpretation of the Malbim commentary on *Yechezkel* 32:15, where the Malbim refers to a pact between the Soviets and the Arabs against Palestine. And the excruciating currentness of that 83rd chapter in *Tehillim*.

The children think this is a TV show. They can't wait for the shooting. They are talking about Migs and Mirages and firepower and tanks and ships as if they were military experts. Where do they pick it all up? They have made toy guns out of wood and they're having war games downstairs.

Today I suggested to Estelle that she and the children leave and I will stay on and join her in the States later. She absolutely refuses. Either we go together, or we stay here together, she says. Her reactions all along have been extremely calm and level-headed. I suspect that most of the Americans who have left, by the way, have done so primarily because their wives are insisting. A man can stand up to one hundred Arab tanks, but it is the rare hero who can stand up to a nagging, frightened wife.

Pressures mount, frustrations deepen, but one aspect of life remains constant and unchanged: Itchkovitch. How does one describe Itchkovitch? It cannot be done. You simply ask, and you receive an answer.

Question: How can a small local shul, designed to house thirty worshippers, hold one thousand worshippers for morning services any day of the week? The answer must be supplied without resorting to the expedient of miracles, the frequency and efficacy of which are already well established in the Holy Land.

Answer: On the corner where Rechov Akiva meets Rechov Rashi in Bnei Brak stands Itchkovitch. The name is a household word. Children learn to say it before they learn mama.

Itchkovitch: If you have slept late one morning after having studied Torah throughout the night, and you want to daven in a shul with a *minyan*, what do you do? If you live anywhere else, you do nothing. You have to pray at home. But if you live in Bnei Brak, what do you do? You go to Itchkovitch. You'll still find a *minyan* there.

If you have not studied Torah the night before and you've gotten up too early for the morning service, what do you do? If you live anywhere in the world, you wait until the right time, and then you go to shul and pray with the *minyan*. But if you live in Bnei Brak, what do you do? You go to Itchkovitch. You'll find a *minyan* there.

Itchkovitch is really not Itchkovitch. It is in fact Congregation Tiferes Tzvi, a small, converted store outfitted with an *Aron Kodesh*, several *Sifrei Torah*, *siddurim*, benches — all the appurtenances of a shul. The man who donated his store for use as a shul is no longer living. His name? Tzvi ben Moshe Itchkovitch. There are other shuls in Israel which are also the result of one man's generosity. But somehow only this, through some mysterious chemistry of fate, is destined to be known forever after by the donor's name.

Where did you daven today? Itchkovitch.

Where did you daven yesterday? Itchkovitch.

Where will you daven tomorrow? Itchkovitch.

But back to our question: How does Itchkovitch, designed to hold thirty worshippers, hold one thousand worshippers every morning? The answer is that Itchkovitch has a "floating *minyan*."

There are always three or four services going on simultaneously, at various stages of progress.

The first *minyan* of some thirty men may be in the shul itself, concluding the prayers with *Aleinu*; at the same moment a second group is out on the side porch, participating in the Torah reading, a third group has appropriated the ladies' section and is in the midst of its prayers, while a fourth is beyond them out on the sidewalk and the street, just beginning *Shacharis*.

When the inner *minyan* finishes and leaves, *minyan* number two on the porch moves inside; the ladies' section *minyan* moves out to the porch, and the sidewalk-street *minyan* moves into the ladies' section. Meanwhile, back at the sidewalk, a new *minyan* has been formed and has begun its own *Shacharis*.

This goes on every morning of the year from daybreak (four A.M. in the summer) until nine or ten in the morning. Allowing thirty minutes and thirty men for each service, about two hundred and forty men are praying every hour. Thus a minimum of one thousand men pray there every morning.

Not only is the number of worshippers remarkable, but the prayers are never perfunctory and are said with meaning and *kavanah*, as prayers should be said. It may seem to be an assembly line, but it really is a direct line to God.

By the way, the same process takes place every afternoon at *Minchah*, which makes two thousand men a day, but I won't stretch the point. And, incidentally, they have no rabbi. There must be a moral here.

After this evening's services the crowd gathers on the street outside, which is the Union Square of Bnei Brak. All kinds of theories, rumors, debates, arguments. Everyone seems to feel, however, that war is imminent and unavoidable. Most of the people are incensed at the government for waiting this long before reacting to Nasser's challenges. They say that every day that goes by is to Nasser's advantage. They want to act immediately, today, now. They blame Eshkol, or Eshkol's wife, or U Thant, or Johnson, or DeGaulle, or each other.

It must have been the conversation, because I slept very little tonight. I kept wondering and imagining what the night holds in store for us. For the first time I was consciously apprehensive. In my imagination I pictured tank battles near Beer Sheba, just ninety minutes away. When I awoke it was six-thirty and the daylight was brilliant in the room, the sky magnificently blue, almost purple. Odd how the cares of the night fade away by the light of day. But at least I was nervous and frightened last night, so I must be somewhat normal, after all.

In class today the handful of students ask me if they might interrupt to listen to the news broadcasts. I readily consent. I watch their faces as they listen, tense and nervous, glued to one tiny transistor radio.

After the news broadcast they tell me that they cannot concentrate on my lecture and they'd like only to talk about the situation. Dina, sweet and pretty and innocent, asks me, "What will be?"

"*Yihyeh tov*," I say with a smile.

Not satisfied, she persists. "But what will be? I could not sleep all week. My mother is beside herself." Dina has a brother in the Air Force and suddenly she does not seem so naive. There are lines on her face.

"What am I," I say, "a prophet? No one knows what will be. Your opinion is as good as mine, maybe better than mine, since you are Israelis and I am not."

She is still not satisfied: "No, no, no. I want to hear *your* opinion. Just your personal opinion."

Suddenly I drop the flippant tone and get very serious. "I do not know what will be. Anyone who says the situation is not serious is just fooling himself. But one fact you must remember. Israel's history is not a natural one, but a supernatural one. By all the rational standards of history there should be no Jewish people, there should be no Torah, there should be no Israel. But we are a people above and beyond the laws of history. We are unique, our history is unique, our God is unique, our way of life is unique. By all the laws of nature and history a nation surrounded on all sides and outnumbered on all sides and hated on all sides should succumb and should be destroyed. But we are not subject to normal and ordinary rules. So maybe on that ground we can perhaps worry a little less."

They listen very attentively, more than they ever did for a lecture. Perhaps it helps them. It helps me.

Yesterday after *Minchah*, the same knots of people at Itchkovitch. Schwab was very angry, his eyes blazing. "This is not Arab against Jew," he was saying. "This is the U.S. against Russia. If the Sovietim and the Americanim want to fight it out, why must we be the pawn? Always the Jew! In 1936 I ran away from Hitler and came to Israel. In 1948 I fought against the Arabs. In 1956 I was in Sinai and fought there. Now again they are after us. Always Israel, always Israel!"

Waiting in line in the drugstore, I hear a customer ask the druggist for some tranquilizers. As the druggist hands them to her, another woman pipes up: "Tranquilizers? Let me have a dozen, too." And so it goes down the line. Everybody suddenly decides that he needs tranquilizers.

According to the news broadcast, the *New York Times* reports that the U.S. did inform Nasser that it might use force against him. The gloom turns to optimism. If the wildest rumor turns up in the *Times* as fact, then nothing is sacred; what comfort can there be in rumors when they become true? Maybe I shouldn't have scoffed at the Sixth Fleet reports.

An interesting item: A young woman has a baby boy in Tel Aviv. Her husband is at the front, deep inside the desert. The *bris* was to have been today, so the army brought the baby and the mother and the *mohel* to the front, and the *bris* took place out there under the hot sun in the sprawling sand, right beside a tank.

The long-anticipated letter from the U.S. Embassy in Israel arrived today. It urges us to leave the country by the next available commercial airliner. It drives home firmly the situation. They are even willing to lend us money if we don't have the means to leave right now. "Well," says my brother Aharon, "surely now you'll go."

Now we have to formulate a new kind of reply to the eternal question: *Atem lo borchim* — You are not fleeing? It is this: "No, not until they send us an aircraft carrier to pick us up right off the Tel Aviv coast. And not just an ordinary carrier. We want a brand new one, with a kosher kitchen." This gets a few laughs. Very few.

I almost overlooked the big news today. During the morning, the civil-defense people distributed leaflets. How to sandbag around the house, how to tape up the windows, how to protect against blasts, what to do during an air raid. A warden in charge of our block has been appointed. He came to the house today to check everything out. He is very solemn and takes the job very seriously. Good for him.

When the children come home from school at noon they are

conscripted into service around our building. They are to help with the sandbagging and in cleaning out the shelter under the building and putting it in order.

People have been storing junk and old furniture down there for years. Out it goes. Our twelve-year-old, Ilan, helps sweep the shelter out and stock it with some water and food. The younger ones, Amram and Jonathan, shovel up all the loose dirt and scurry about looking for bags to fill. They run in and out of the apartment and get on our nerves in their excitement. They want water, and string, and hammers, and screwdrivers, and brooms. They have enough equipment to defeat an Arab army. They haven't had so much fun since they saw the Braves in a double-header last spring in Atlanta. The Braves: how far away all that is.

Chavah, almost seven, comes in and wants to know, "Abba, what is a bomb?"

"A bomb is something that can hurt you."

"I know, I know. Do you think I'm a baby? But what *is* a bomb?"

"It falls from an airplane and it makes a big noise when it hits the ground and you'd better not be around if one falls. That's what the shelter is for. That's what a bomb is."

"Is a bomb like a bullet?"

"Yes, something like a bullet, only bigger."

"Will the Arabs drop a bomb on us?"

"I don't know. I hope not."

"Will they drop a bomb on Israel?"

"Maybe, maybe not."

"Will God let the Arabs drop a bomb on Israel?"

I am on the spot. "Well, I hope He won't let them."

"Israel is a holy country. You said so. Will God let the Arabs hurt a holy country?"

Why do the righteous suffer? Iyov, R. Akiva: I am caught. "I don't know, Chav. I don't know what God will do. But I don't think God will let us get hurt, so don't you worry."

"Well, if God won't let us get hurt, why do we need to get the shelter ready?"

I mumble something about eating lunch.

Later this afternoon, I came across a remarkable law in *Orach Chaim*, section 574, paragraph 5: "He who separates himself from the community will not witness their comfort and will not witness their consolation; but he who joins with the community in their sorrow and trouble will be deemed worthy to see their consolation." One of the commentators on the text adds this interesting gloss: Joining in the sorrow of the community means that one must actively do something to help the community's problems. Just being around and doing nothing is not considered joining in a community's sorrow.

This seems to be written just for me. I had better go out and do something active to help out. Certainly writing this diary is doing no one any real good.

I heard today about a yeshiva student who is spending all his time this week studying the *halachos* of "Sanctification of the Name," which deals with proper conduct at the time of death in order to sanctify the Name of God. "In case an Arab wants to kill me, I'll know exactly how to behave," he says quite simply.

When I arrive at the huge Ponevezh Yeshiva on Friday night for services, I find the entire building completely sandbagged. How incongruous: a place of Torah and of peace and of study and of learning on a war footing. And the motto inscribed at the top of the building, in large black Hebrew letters, "*Ul'har habayis yihyeh pleitah* — And the Temple Mount shall be for a refuge." It hits me with new force. It is said that the Ponevezher Rav, the famous dean of the Yeshiva, chose this inscription because the saintly Chafetz Chaim had said, in 1936, that there would be a second world war but that Palestine would be spared. He had based his statement on this passage from *Yeshayahu*.

The students had worked all day on the sandbagging. The bearded ones, their *tzitzis* flapping, the ascetic students — all had joined in the work with deep religious fervor. In the main study hall itself there is no electricity for *Maariv*, only a few kerosene lamps hanging from the walls. It casts an eerie mixture of light and shadow throughout the hall.

Since most buildings here are without screens, birds are constantly flying around the ceilings of libraries, auditoriums, classrooms. Tonight birds fly through the huge windows of the Ponevezh *beis midrash* and chirp on the light fixtures high above, their tiny heads bobbing up and down. Others prefer the antique, burnished *Aron Kodesh* which was once housed in an old Italian synagogue. They swoop into the carefully wrought crevices and make their nests above the crouching lions, next to the Ten Commandments.

As on every Friday night, Rav Chatzkel Levenstein delivers the *mussar shmuess* to the students. The benches are all clustered around the front of the Ark, and you must come several hours before he begins in order to reserve a place. And if you are late, you stand. You have to strain to hear him, for he is eighty-five, his voice no longer carries more than a few yards, and he speaks in a kind of hoarse whisper. His role at Ponevezh is that of spiritual mentor and guide to the six hundred students, and his Friday night talks center around issues of man, and God, and Torah. Abstract subjects? Yes.

But his *shmuessen* attract not only every student, but several hundred local rabbis and scholars as well. In America, people fight for seats to a football game; in Bnei Brak they fight to get a seat to hear Reb Chatzkel.

His words are deeply moving. The ongoing crisis, he says, is very serious. Nothing that happens to us is simply accidental. All is from above, directed from on high. He cites *Devarim* 30:19: "I have set before you life and death, the blessing and the curse. Therefore choose life…" God gives man the freedom to choose his own path. But he places before men the opportunity of coming closer to God, *hiskarvus*. We must not regard anything as purely accidental, or coincidental. God presents us daily with opportunities which we can utilize to achieve attachment to Him. We can, if we choose, ignore these opportunities and walk along whistling a pretty tune. But he who has eyes to see and ears to hear knows that nothing is by chance. Everything is part of a grand design.

Reb Chatzkel's figure sways gently to and fro. The evening sky grows dark outside. The kerosene lamps cast a bronze glow over the students. Even Reb Chatzkel's face, usually white, is now glowing. His black hat, his black suit, have disappeared in the darkness. Only his face, narrow and gaunt, is visible. And his white beard. His bent shadow darts up and down the *Aron Kodesh* behind him. His audience is still, some eyes tightly closed in an effort to concentrate, others wide open in wonder, still others swaying intently to and fro.

What we face, he continues, is serious, extremely serious. But its gravity is not only the physical danger that confronts us, but the spiritual opportunity as well. All this — the mobilization, the emergency, the danger — has not occurred haphazardly. It is an opportunity for us to cleave to God, to achieve *hiskarvus*. He who is aware of the ways of God will leap at the opportunity. He who is blind will stumble. God wants to bring the Jewish people closer to Him, and so He has placed before us the situation with which this can be achieved. He who will wake up and look — he will come close to God. He who will remain asleep will not only not come close; he will be farther away than ever before.

We hear a great deal about faith in God. Have faith — all will be well. This is not faith. Faith is achieved through hard work, through prayer, through study of Torah, through performance of God's *mitzvos*. To walk through the streets unconcerned, to have full confidence that God will make everything come out all right — this is not faith. This is child's play. Our men are in the deserts suffering in the heat of day and the cold of night. They are away from home, from wife and children. They face death at any moment. Are we to whistle a pretty tune and say quite calmly, Don't worry, all will be well? An emergency like this is supposed to bend us a little, make us a little less proud, a little less self-assured, a little more aware of God's role in the world.

Perhaps God has set before us this crisis in order to give us the chance for *hiskarvus*. Perhaps God wants us to pray to Him because He has seen that we have drifted far from Him. Let us not walk around with foolish and empty rationalizations and theories. Let us react to crisis as Jews react. Not with false bravado, not with foolish optimism, but rather with the knowledge that nothing is by chance, and that nothing simply "happens."

It is easy to say, Have faith. But faith is saying that whatever God does I will accept as His will. We must ask ourselves if we are ready to give our lives for *kiddush HaShem* if we are called upon to do so. We must be ready to suffer for His Name. "You shall love Hashem your God with all your heart, with all your soul, with all your might." "With all your might" means that even in the face of torture worse than death we must be ready to love God and to serve Him. This is the faith which is appropriate in this hour.

The *Maariv* that follows in the darkened study hall is a passionate one. Six hundred strong, praying with the kind of fervor that one expects but only rarely sees on a Yom Kippur evening. The intensity, the devotion, the fervor are so deep, the cries so loud, and the swaying to and fro so violent — and these are young men, not aged women — that one is willy-nilly caught up in it with them. No one can watch this kind of scene objectively and from a distance.

There is a long preparatory pause before they say *Shema*, then a sudden explosion: again six hundred voices chant "*Shema Yisrael*, Hear O Israel, Hashem is our God, Hashem is One"; six hundred voices crying out, "*Hishamru lachem* — Beware lest you turn aside and serve other gods and worship them, and Hashem's anger will be kindled against you ... and you will perish quickly from the good land which Hashem gives you": a tremble as you say it, and a shudder as you hear the others say it.

If prayer is to be said with fear and awe and trembling, then tonight it has been done, because fear, awe, and trembling are real and palpable and tangible.

The children and I walk home through the quiet, darkened street and we have our Shabbos meal. Everyone tries to be cheerful, and the children of course are not really worried about anything: since the good guy always wins and Israel is the good guy how can there be a problem? After we sing *zemiros* and other songs (I am particularly moved by the song from *Shemoneh Esrei*, "You are the beneficent One whose mercy has never ceased, You are the merciful One whose kindness has never ended, and forever and ever do we hope in You") we recite *Birkas Hamazon* and go out for a stroll on Rechov Akiva.

Very few people are out tonight, and even those who are walking somehow do not have the usual serene Shabbos look. The tension has even invaded and violated the day of peace. We meet Rabbi Leiner, who has lived in Israel for forty years. He tells us that never has he seen such universal gloom. "Even in 1948, when things were bad, it was better than this. Never have I seen them so pessimistic, so universally discouraged — everyone's face is black."

The air is filled with predictions tonight: It's too quiet; they can't keep it up, just keeping all those soldiers at the front; there's bound to be an explosion at any moment. Nagler, the tall, two-hundred-forty pounder from Brooklyn who has settled in Israel and wears a *shtreimel* and long *kapotte* and is all but indistinguishable from a native Chassid, tells me confidentially that the Hungarian Circus performers who have been putting on a nightly show in Tel Aviv were caught this week by the *Shin-Bet* — the Israeli F. B. I. — "their crates filled with enough weapons to blow up all the country." He claims that they were immediately deported and that the whole matter has been hushed up. How does he know? "Believe me, believe me, I know, I know," he says with a reassuring smile.

17 Iyar

Shabbos, May 27

WAKE UP THIS MORNING at four-thirty, a distant rumble in my ears. Artillery? I strain to listen. More of it. I get up to look out the window. It is quiet and peaceful. I go back to bed. I hear more rumbling. I get up and look out the back window. The night sky is still. Back to bed again. And then, fully awake, I realize that it is our upstairs neighbor moving his furniture around. At four-thirty in the morning! Who's nervous?

I leave the apartment with the children at about six-thirty in the morning to go to Ponevezh for services. On the way we meet Bura, towel in hand, returning from the *mikveh*. He tells me that Israel would have attacked last night but that we postponed it for certain technical reasons. It will most certainly take place tonight. "They simply cannot keep the boys at the front this long and not give them something to do. The soldiers are champing at the bit."

Of all the rumor-mongers around, I put most stock in Bura because he is simply not the rumor type. I am sure that he has some fairly valid sources. But during the day I do not repeat any of what he has told me. Let people enjoy their Shabbos as best they can.

In the shuls of Bnei Brak today there appeared a reprint of an old letter written by the Chazon Ish, who was considered, until his death twelve years ago, the most outstanding authority in Jewish law in the world today. He was one of the truly great saints of the last five hundred years. During the siege of Jerusalem in 1948 when the inhabitants of the city were all but starved out, he had written them a letter encouraging them and urging them to remain steadfast and strong and not to abandon the Holy City during the bombardment. Rather, he wrote, they must increase their learning of Torah and their practice of the *mitzvos*. This is the entire text of that letter from the Chazon Ish which is now posted on every shul wall and on every kiosk in Bnei Brak:

> It is necessary to strengthen one's self in the study of Torah in order to increase the merit of all of us, generally and particularly, and this is better than fasting and the like. Of course, there should be learning for the purpose of doing, particularly should one now be most careful about the "you shall not" *mitzvos*, since people violate these more easily. Specifically, those *mitzvos* dealing with the relations of man and his fellow man. We should now be most cautious not to cause any sorrow to our fellow man for the slightest instant, even through an inadvertent remark, for this would be a specific violation of a Torah commandment, as the Talmud states.

18 Iyar

Sunday, May 28

THERE WAS NO ATTACK last night, not by the Israelis, not by the Egyptians. I get the feeling that Bura is avoiding me today.

Today, by the way, is *Lag Ba'omer*. The Vizhnitzer Rebbe is said to have made the statement that on *Lag Ba'omer* "the enemies of Israel will be destroyed"; and there are reports of the will left by the famous shoemaker of Tel Aviv, who just passed away a few months ago. He was a very pious man — not a rabbi — who was so highly regarded by the great rabbis of Israel that they would ask him to pray for them. Even the Chazon Ish, it is said, used to ask the shoemaker — or "*der shuster,*" as he was known — to pray on his behalf. Now it is said that in his will was a sealed envelope which was not to be opened until just before *Lag Ba'omer*. It was opened this past week and in it was a letter stating that at this season the enemies of Israel will raise their heads, there will be days of utter darkness, and Israel will emerge in great triumph.

Late in the afternoon I am sitting in the Bar Ilan library preparing my lecture for tomorrow. The male students are all mobilized, the female students are all doing volunteer work, but the classes are officially still in session. Saul Kress comes over to me and asks me what I plan to do. Saul, very quiet and reserved, is a professor of chemistry at Columbia, and has come to teach in Israel just for one year. He is supposed to leave in August, but during the past week has been off-again-on-again about leaving immediately. A few days ago he made definite plans to leave with his wife and four children and then for some reason changed his mind. When I saw him last on Thursday he had decided irrevocably to stay, come what may. Now, the irrevocable has evidently been revoked. He tells me that he must leave, but he doesn't tell me the reason, only that he is very nervous about staying. I know the real reason. His wife is a concentration camp survivor and simply cannot take the strain and tension of these days. He is leaving tomorrow and wishes me well. He tells me all this in a matter-of-fact way. No apologies about leaving, no weasel excuses. He is leaving like a man. The other visiting professors from America and England who have left during this past week have all done so almost under cover of darkness, surreptitiously, guiltily, with all kinds of excuses, none of which includes the fact that they themselves are frightened. As if fear is something to be ashamed of, as if it is an emotion reserved only for women. Why do men somehow think that fear is beneath them? Always it's "my wife is insisting that we go," or "I have to do it for the kids." All of which is true, but not one of them has had the good sense to admit that he himself is also scared. Only Saul. As a matter of fact, I am coming to the conclusion that it takes as much bravery for an honest man to leave Israel these days as it does for him to stay.

But Saul saves the best for the end. "How long have you been sitting here?" he asks.

"About three hours," I say.

"Well, about an hour ago they were looking for some Arab infiltrators who have been laying mines all over the area. The army and the police are looking for them right now, and they were just swarming all over the campus about half an hour ago. They haven't found them yet. It's getting dark and I'd suggest you don't wait too long before you go home."

"All right," I say. "We'll go together."

We walk out into the campus. The sunset, as usual, is dazzling as it lights up the clouds in a thousand shades of blue and pink and orange and purple. The campus is deserted.

"Looks quiet," I say.

"Yes. But don't walk on the grass. Stay on the concrete. Don't pick anything up, and when you drive watch out for any unusual objects in the road."

He is jittery! I get gingerly into the car and drive carefully — and nervously — home. When I walk into the apartment, Ilan asks me how things were at Bar Ilan. "Oh, fine, just fine."

19 Iyar

Monday, May 29

ODAY I AM STANDING in a bookstore and the lady in front of me leans over the counter and whispers ominously to the proprietor: "Are you ready?"

"Ready for what?"

"You know, your house. You have enough food? You have to get ready, you know. There is definitely going to be a war."

She speaks in a very authoritative and confidential tone, but she is only a housewife who lives down the block. She is doing her little bit to keep things calm.

Estelle reports that today at the new supermarket there was a near riot over the few boxes of stale Passover matzos which were still left on the shelves. The stores are limiting customers to two small boxes per person, and one woman grabbed about six or seven. This upset everyone since matzos are a prime food during a shortage: they don't spoil and they are filling. The poor woman who had taken all those matzos was beleaguered by the rest. One woman yelled at her, *"Halo, anachnu kulanu Yehudim?* Are we not all Jews?" Estelle was very disturbed at the spectacle. P.S. Unwilling to do battle over them, she brought home no matzos at all. There is no question that if the war should break out, or if even just a serious shortage should occur, our kitchen will be unique: it is the least stocked in all Israel.

As the crisis tightens a notch each day, the latent religiosity of the average Israeli becomes more apparent. With the vehicle shortage, I pick up hitchhikers constantly and can't help plying them with questions in order to gain some insight into their thinking. Among the pious, God is mentioned more frequently; among the non-pious, He is now mentioned occasionally, albeit haltingly and self-consciously. Although some of Israel's Jews have tried to maintain the spurious and cliched philosophy of I-don't-need-religion-and-its-observances-the-land-of-Israel-is-my-religion-and-my-God, this somehow is insufficient right now, and everyone seems to feel this. There are no atheists in foxholes, true, and I suppose anyone in trouble turns to religion quite automatically. But these are militant anti-religionists I am talking about, who had carefully worked out a philosophy of non-religion. But I should not be surprised at this development. Can one generation really erase four thousand years of God-consciousness?

The most amazing — and comforting — of all are the Yemenite Jews. One woman hitched a ride with me this morning. In her utter simplicity she did not realize how profound she was, and that she was echoing the words of Reb Chatzkel. "Whatever God does, whether it is good or whether it is bad, we should be ready to accept it. God is good, and I trust in Him to do what has to be done, even if to us it might seem bad." She went on to tell me that she had lost a son in the Suez campaign in 1956, and that now her younger son is in the army.

Crises have a cleansing effect and one of the items swept away is prejudice. Israelis in general are rather prejudiced against the so-called "ultra-pious" of Bnei Brak. It was only three weeks ago that I was riding in a taxi and the driver turned to me and asked, "Are you from America?"

My Hebrew "R" is so smooth and clean, tripping off my lips instead of rolling down in the throat where it belongs; I was reading the English-language *Jerusalem Post*; I was wearing American-style clothes.

"Are you from America?"

"Well, yes."

"Ah, you are from Brooklyn?" with the accent on the "lyn."

"No."

"Where then?"

"From the South. From the Negev."

"Ah, Texas? Are there many oil wells?"

I have learned to be patient. "No, not Texas."

"And are you a tourist here?"

"Not exactly. We are staying here for a year."

"And where do you live?"

I paused for effect. I looked him straight in the eye. I said it slowly, watching his face. "I live in Bnei Brak."

"Bnei Brak, that is a very religious place." He looked at me again, newly. He did not have to tell me what he was thinking, but he did: "Why should a modern, up-to-date American want to live in Bnei Brak?"

The taxi driver is not unusual. My conversation with him and his reaction is a kind of game that repeats itself regularly. For most Israelis, Bnei Brak is synonymous with *shtreimlach*, *peyos*, long beards, long black *kapottes*, black, broad-brimmed hats, furtive women with wigs, long-sleeved dresses. Israelis — and not only the secular ones — call Bnei Brak Jews fanatics. "Is it really necessary to walk around that way?" a storekeeper in Tel Aviv asks me. "All that is so European, so typically *Galus*. Who needs it? You don't have to go around like that in order to be religious." And at the university, a fellow teacher, himself rather observant, says to me: "Those *kapottes* and *shtreimlach* — they copied those clothes from the Middle Ages, from the *goyim*. There is nothing holy about them. They are only the clothes of wealthy Polish landowners."

I have found that the more liberal a man thinks he is, the more is he prejudiced against these Bnei Brak Jews; the more emancipated he thinks he is, the more do these people disturb him. It is as if his liberality and his emancipated status were threatened by those who stubbornly maintain the ancient forms. I once pointed out to one of these liberals that he is in a kind of spiritual league with Hitler, for Hitler, too, could not tolerate the sight of those fur hats and long black coats and long beards and *peyos*, and he tried to obliterate them all. For me it is a vindication of that wonderful stubbornness of the Jew to see him walking around Bnei Brak wearing the very same clothes which his powerful oppressor hated so bitterly.

But all this is now changed — at least for the duration. It is amazing what the crisis has done for unity in this country. Only a few weeks ago Israel was in the midst of a bitter *kulturkampf* between the religious and the secularist elements, with the current battle lines drawn over the issue of indiscriminate autopsies.

86

But now even the *Jerusalem Post*, which usually goes out of its way to cast aspersions on the religious elements in Israel, is going out of its way to show how the religious Jews are aiding the mobilization effort. The other day they ran a feature on some yeshiva boys in Jerusalem who, though they were exempt from army duty, were nevertheless donating blood, helping sandbag the buildings, and volunteering for all kinds of onerous work. Today they ran a long feature story on an Air Force pilot who wears his *yarmulke* under his flight helmet. On Shabbos, he flew his normal reconnaisance mission. After landing at the airfield, the Air Force sent out a bus to pick up the pilots and take them back to the dining room. He refused to ride with them and walked the two miles alone. "What I have to do, I do — and I have to fly my plane even on Shabbos. But I do not have to ride to the mess hall, so I walk." In normal times the *Post* would probably have laughed at this "fanatic," but now they give us his picture and a long, glowing article about his principles and beliefs. Let's hope that all of this good will does not evaporate along with the crisis. And let's hope that the crisis evaporates and does not explode.

There is a new status symbol for Americans in Israel. When we meet one another we try to compare how many frantic telegrams and letters we have received from our families and friends in the United States. A telegram counts for five points, a special delivery letter is three points, and a normally frantic letter counts for two points.

Oh, yes, how could I forget? Letters. Today I walk into the main Bnei Brak post office and tell the clerk on the main floor that I would like to offer my services and that of my car to the post office. He eyes me suspiciously.

"Not my department," he says very curtly. "Ask him," pointing to the lone clerk sitting in the far corner.

I go over to "him" and repeat my offer. Though he knows me quite well, he looks me over from head to toe several times. I am beginning to feel like a criminal. Then he smiles.

"Very nice, very nice. But that is not my department. Please go upstairs and speak to the *menahel*."

The sound of the word *menahel* almost makes me reel. Every tiny office in Israel, every business, every school, every factory, every two-bit operation has its *menahel*. Literally it means "director" or "manager." In actual fact, it refers to the chief bureaucrat, chief pencil-pusher, chief red-taper, who is usually a small, narrow-eyed, suspicious, green-visored monster who has waited twenty-five years to attain his exalted position and is not about to let *you* tell *him* anything. If he is drinking tea while you and twelve other people are waiting humbly in line to see him, you wait. Tea comes first. And tea comes at ten and at three — *b'diyuk*, punctually, come hell or high water — or Nasser. It is no wonder that Israel is in the midst of a recession. Israel is full of *menahelim*, they are all drinking tea, and all work comes to a thirty-minute standstill twice a day, *b'diyuk*, six days a week. After tea-drinking time, you are ushered into his sanctum sanctorum, you state your case politely and you genuflect with your words, you pay obeisance as to a king, you wait on his every word and you depart quickly. He is, after all, the *menahel*, and you are simply a lowly member of the public, and in a country which bears the Russian-Turkish-British tradition of the-public-be-damned, you had better learn quickly your place in the scheme of things, which places you down at the bottom and the *menahel* up at the top.

And I have to see the *menahel*! With all my noble motives about helping out, with all my willingness to volunteer time and energy and whatever is necessary to do my share, I confess that at the sound of the word I almost forget about the crisis and go home. But — and this must surely be the single most valorous act of the entire crisis for which I am the unsung hero of Israel — I throw out my chest, walk upstairs, knock bravely on the *menahel*'s door, and wait.

"Come in, come in!" comes an impatient voice.

He is sitting behind his desk. He is little, fat, bald-headed, narrow-eyed: my caricature is real.

"Yes," he says, trying to sound haughty. "What can I do for you?"

"I know that you are short of people and of vehicles. I would like to volunteer my services, and I also have a car that I could put at your disposal if you want it."

"You realize, of course, that we will not pay for your gasoline?"

I am momentarily stunned, and mumble something quite unintelligible.

"Well then, in that case we can certainly use you. Come over here and sit down at my desk."

While he has not yet stepped down from his high seat of judgment, I feel that I have been elevated from my lowly status. He has offered me a seat at his desk. And now he breaks out into a real smile.

"You know," he continues, "we have here a fleet of eleven mail trucks. Ten of them are now in the Sinai desert. We have one truck doing the work of eleven right now. But that is not all. That one truck broke down yesterday and we are left just with one bicycle. Today we tried to get that truck fixed but every mechanic in Israel seems to be in the Sinai desert as well. So we are delivering frantic telegrams and special delivery letters and ordinary mail to 80,000 inhabitants of this area with that one decrepit old bicycle. My friend, you could not have come at a better time." And he extends his right hand and gives me a warm handshake.

I bask for a glorious moment in my new-found equality. Some Israelis live for one hundred and twenty years and never experience the hand of a real *menahel* extended to them in friendship. I have truly arrived. My friends in my building will not believe this.

"When do I begin?"

"Can you be here tomorrow morning at seven o'clock?"

"I'll see you then."

And thus begins my career as a volunteer driver. I am looking forward to it. It will be useful work, and while it promises to be dull and prosaic, it has already been rewarding: a genuine *menahel* has smiled at me.

An Israeli woman returned to Bnei Brak today from New York. She claims that things are much calmer here than there. She says the American Jewish community is in a state of complete hysteria and frustration, and does not quite know what to do or how to help other than to raise funds and issue protests. She maintains that it is a pleasure to be back in Israel where things are so peaceful. But with this crisis costing Israel a million dollars a day, fund-raising should perhaps not be ridiculed. Nor protests, either.

The discipline in Bnei Brak among the pious Jews is remarkable. Each one runs to his rabbi to ask a *she'eilah* about whether he should or should not leave the country. Each one wants to know the *daas Torah*, and not leave such a fateful decision to himself. For the Torah-oriented Jew no area in life is acted upon without getting the

Torah point of view, which is represented by the *Gadol*, the leading scholar of the community. It is a kind of military discipline which enables them to follow in full faith the instructions of their rabbi. What are the rabbis advising? You get conflicting reports, but most of them are apparently telling the Americans not to leave and that they must stay and take part in the *eis tzarah*, the time of peril.

The radio today reports that about one hundred yeshiva boys from America have arrived in Israel to assist in the crisis. In general, the Israeli population is very much encouraged by the great support — although it is primarily verbal so far — of the Jews of the western world, as well as what is apparently the support of general public opinion in the West. But we are still anxious because the governments are reacting quite differently.

Conflicting emotions still bear down upon us: fear of war, bombing, injury; fear of possible rationing, standing in line, ensuing human ugliness and selfishness; the closing of airports and harbors. And then there is pride which co-mingles with the fear. *Al tifrosh min hatzibur:* shame at leaving Israel behind while it is in trouble; shame at facing others in the United States; shame at facing one's own self if we leave now. Shame is a powerful emotion: it overcomes fear. And since *melo kol haaretz kevodo*, and since, like Yonah, where can one run from Him, should not one stay here in any case? And should not one be part of *tzaras Klal Yisrael*?

In this kind of crisis the strong grow weak, the weak strong.

In connection with my ruminations above, I just remembered *Yirmeyahu* 42. In verse 14, the prophet says:

> But if you say, We will not remain in this land so as not to hearken to the voice of Hashem your God, saying, no; but into the land of Egypt will we go, that we may not see war, nor hear the

sound of the horn, and that we may not have hunger for bread and there will we dwell.

And he goes on to say:

If you will indeed set your faces to enter into Egypt, and go there to sojourn there, then shall the sword, of which you are afraid, there overtake you in the land of Egypt and the famine, whereof you are in dread, shall there cleave close unto you in Egypt, and there shall you die.

In other words, there is simply no escaping God. It may seem odd, but that thundering 42nd chapter of *Yirmeyahu* is a comforting thought these days.

These are great days of testing. The special daily chapters of *Tehillim* and the *Avinu Malkenu* prayer are holding back the oncoming storm by force. The posters of the rabbis keep appearing on the walls and they call for repentance, increased learning, increased charity, and increased awareness of God. And the passages in the regular daily prayers that suddenly come to life, passages that I have been saying every single day of my life but haven't really heard or listened to until now: *Al tivtechu binedivim*, do not trust in princes; and in *Shemoneh Esrei, ki goel chazak Atah*, You are our mighty redeemer; and the recurring phrases in *Birkas Hamazon, tamid lo chasar lanu v'al yechsar lanu mazon*, never shall we be in want of food; *eretz chemdah tovah urchavah*, a good and lovely land.

Life at the university — at least on the surface — goes on as if nothing has changed. We have received a notice from the university president to maintain our "normal lecture schedules." Almost all the boys have been called up, and those who have not been called — as well as most of the girls — have taken volunteer jobs in hospitals, or farms, or schools. Half the faculty is gone, and the few students who come to class have their minds elsewhere. But we are to maintain our "normal lecture schedules," so we go through the motions. But our heart is not in it.

I wonder where Rachamim is, and how he is doing.

Eshkol's radio talk to the nation yesterday was a debacle. Apparently without a prepared text in front of him, he hemmed and hawed and stammered, and muttered unintelligible asides. If his words were calculated to inspire confidence, they had the opposite effect. Thank God there's no TV in the country; at least we were spared the ordeal of watching it. He was almost incoherent. I had to resort to today's papers to find out what he actually said. No one can argue with his sentiments. Israel, he said, would fight if necessary for freedom of passage through the Straits of Tiran. He called the blockade an aggressive act and said that Israel's army was ready to defend itself. Who can disagree with that? It is clear and forthright and necessary. But, oh, what his delivery has done to our morale! This is our leader. He sounded like a *bobbe*. I only hope the soldiers at the front were not able to hear him.

There have been all kinds of murmurings against Eshkol these past weeks, and much of it has been the natural result of the current frustration and tension. But this radio address has already become the topic of conversation wherever you go. People say, "Did you hear Eshkol yesterday?" and smile feebly, utter a half-groan, and sadly shake their heads. The image projected by Eshkol has always been one of stodginess, dullness, heavy-footedness. Now that image is reinforced, and there will be no shaking it off.

20 Iyar

Tuesday, May 30

A T THE UNIVERSITY THIS morning I ran into Schwartz of the director's office. After the usual preliminaries (You are not leaving? and my usual reply) he sighed deeply and shook his head: "*Oy*, is that an Eshkol. Did you hear him yesterday? What a *yente*. I tell you we need to get rid of him. We need Ben Gurion in there, or Dayan. Someone who knows how to make a decision. Someone who knows how to inspire. All this man can do is *krechtz*. It's not good, I tell you, not good."

And so it was wherever I went today. A growing clamor to get rid of Eshkol, a growing mood of irritation. And, with a desperation born of despair — even the two words are fundamentally the same — some of the newspapers are now openly calling for Ben Gurion to return to the government. And almost all of them are demanding that Dayan serve in some capacity.

It is not all bad, however. The country has been laughing all day ever since the news came in that three Egyptian army officers and two privates were captured on the Israeli side of the Egyptian border. They were in an Egyptian patrol car. According to the radio, the Egyptian soldiers claim that they got lost and took a wrong turn in the road. Instead of turning west, they turned east, right into the arms of an Israeli patrol. As usual, say the Israelis, they are going the wrong way. Are they coming or going, say others. Poor, downtrodden jokes, but it does help to laugh at one's enemy, even if the jokes at his expense are rather shopworn.

How could I forget? I worked all day as a mailman. I delivered special delivery letters and telegrams, and noticed that almost all of them were from the United States and were delivered to Americans here. One does not have to be a Sherlock Holmes to deduce the nature of the messages: Come home!

During the day I also had to drive one of the regular postmen all over the area to pick up mail from the various boxes which have not been emptied for over a week. As we stopped near one corner, one of his friends yelled out to him: "Look at you, Chaim. American car, American chauffeur. Big shot. Even Eshkol doesn't drive around in such style." We had a hearty laugh.

I go back on duty tomorrow. It is rather dull work, but it is necessary work, and at least I no longer feel parasitic; and now I have a new answer to the eternal question of why we are not leaving: What? And let the post office flounder without me?

There was a report today that two Liberian ships are on the high seas, carrying cargo to Eilat. They are due to pass into the Gulf of Aqaba in the next forty-eight hours. If true — and each news report carries a slightly different version and no one seems to know where the report originated — but if true, zero hour is approaching. It reminds me of the Cuban crisis: Soviet ships approaching Cuba, America laying down a blockade — I think the word we used then was quarantine — and everyone holding his breath. This is a kind of High Noon situation. Nasser cannot permit the ships to go through the Straits of Tiran to Israel; Israel cannot afford to have the ships turned back or fired at.

And so we wait.

What will come of this? Somehow, in some way, the blockade will have to be run. And then — who knows?

21 Iyar

Wednesday, May 31

TODAY I SAW A reprint of an editorial in *Al-Ahram*, Nasser's mouthpiece. It is rather grim: "There is no alternative to armed conflict between the U.A.R. and the Israeli enemy." And Israel radio is reporting Nasser's daily press conferences. Today, for example, Nasser said that he has in the last week restored the situation to what it was before 1956. Now, he says, "God will help us restore the situation to what it was prior to 1948." Clear enough. Prior to 1948 there was no Israel, period. Of course, Nasser and the Arabs use language differently than we do. They get very emotionally involved and tied up in their own rhetoric. The more fancies they spin out the more they believe them. It is a kind of unreality which in itself becomes reality. Although we are by now familiar with their bombast, this is different. Nasser's bombast is backed up, we hear, by six infantry and armored divisions and nine hundred tanks — and the latest Russian equipment. As never before, the Arabs seem united against Israel. Russia must be behind all of this. Nasser would not dare otherwise.

It does seem to me — and the feeling is universal here — that Israel has no alternative but to fight. Where in the history of the world has a nation reacted passively to a blockade of a major port? The patience of Israel is incredible and can only be the result of some promises which Johnson must have made to Eban in Washington last week. But things simply cannot go on like this. The people are chafing at the humiliation of not reacting. They feel they have lost the initiative and that each day they wait is in Nasser's favor. Every newspaper is clamoring for action, and the calls for Dayan and Ben Gurion are increasing in intensity.

Bombshell: I am walking toward Itchkovitch for *Minchah* when I run into our neighbor, Mr. Herman. His face, usually full of cheer, is sagging.

"Anything new?" I ask.

"You haven't heard the news?"

"What news?"

"About Hussein. About Jordan."

"No. Tell me."

He sighs as only a Jew can sigh. Two thousand years of persecution are in that sigh. "Hussein just made a pact with Nasser. He flew into Cairo today. Now Jordan is also involved."

"Well," I try to comfort, "Jordan is so tiny they wouldn't dare. And Hussein is really a moderate. It's not so terrible."

"Not so terrible! Do you know who their soldiers are? The Arab Legion! Trained by the British. The best soldiers the Arabs have. Professionals. Ah," he groans, "this is a world, such a world."

At Itchkovitch, Hussein is the main subject of conversation. At the end of *Minchah*, we read *Tehillim* 83 with new meaning:

> Against Your people they shrewdly take counsel, and they plot against those whom You protect. They have said, "Come and let us cut them off from being a nation, so the name of Israel shall be remembered no more." When they plot in their heart together, against You they make a covenant — the tents of Edom and the Ishmaelites, Moav and Hagrim; Geval and Ammon and Amalek, the Philistines with the inhabitants of Tyre.

We are really surrounded now: Egypt, Syria, Lebanon, and now Jordan. And this does not include Iraq, Sudan, Algeria, and Kuwait. The names in 1967 may be somewhat altered from those of David's times in 1,000 B.C.E., but the name of the game is the same: kill the Jew, let us cut them off from being a nation.

Later in the evening I hear the details on the news program. It is not good. Iraq has sent a complete division to Egypt and put it at Nasser's disposal. Others of her troops are now entering Jordan.

And the world? More statements and pronouncements about maritime powers, and restraint, and freedom of navigation, and sovereignty of nations. In English translation all this means only one thing: the world is perfectly unconcerned about the prospect of two and one-half million additional Jews being put to the slaughter. Six million in Europe were not enough. I wonder if the Deputy at the Vatican is already documenting his facts to prove, in 1975, that he was *not* silent in May of 1967.

Today's despairing mood was somewhat lifted late tonight. We heard a radio broadcast from the Sinai front on which there were featured various actors and singers entertaining the troops. Listening to the troops laugh at the jokes was exhilarating. And a new song was introduced tonight: *"Anachnu na'avor b'meitzarai Tiran* — We will pass through the Straits of Tiran." The song is rousing, magnificent. Something about having passed through many obstacles in our history: the Red Sea, the River Jordan, and we will pass through Tiran as well. The soldiers sang the chorus hoarsely, lustily. It brought tears to my eyes. There was also a haunting, plaintive melody about Jerusalem of gold, and copper, and light, and the Wailing Wall, and Jericho, and the Dead Sea. After a few stanzas, all the soldiers joined in. Really touching and poignant.

Where else in the world can one listen to the troops being entertained — live? It is kind of unreal to listen at your kitchen radio to the soldiers who are at the front just a few miles away.

Every few hours the radio carries messages to and from the soldiers and their families: "Chaim Zohar's wife and daughters from Ein Hanetziv wish Chaim well and ask him to write." "Yosef Kohen is fine and sends love to his family in Haifa and tells them not to worry, everything is *b'seder.*"

Announcement on the radio today: "Please do not send perishables such as chicken and other foods to your soldiers at the front. They are being well fed by the army. Your food is simply rotting away." Yiddishe Mommes: worrying that their boys do not have enough to eat.

I have written it before, but it is once again true. What seems intolerable and unbearable one day becomes quite acceptable and normal the next. Jordan making a pact with Egypt would have been unthinkable on Monday; on Wednesday it is *déjà vu.*

There is nothing to worry about: the men at Itchkovitch have spoken. I wandered from group to group tonight as they stood arguing on the sidewalk and in the street. As they have done for the past ten days they stand — hundreds of them — in groups of ten or twenty, talking excitedly in Hebrew, Hungarian, Yiddish, Polish, English, arms churning the air, fingers pointing, postulating theories and premises and arriving at rather illogical conclusions. But the men at Itchkovitch have spoken, and by and large they are saying that Hussein will never fight. Firstly, he is a moderate; secondly, he has close ties with the United States, and they will not permit him to do anything rash. Of course, the ominous undertone of the pact is being overlooked: Hussein and Nasser hate each other, and if, despite this, Hussein is climbing the bandwagon, does he know something that makes it necessary for him to fall into Nasser's arms? And does this something point once again to Russia?

Nasser is still rattling his sabers and making wild speeches: "total war," "destruction of Israel." Referring to the new pact with his "brother" Hussein (whom he recently called "the Jordanian prostitute") he said today, "The Arabs are ready for battle. The hour of decision has arrived." Let us hope that this is the usual bluster.

Well, Aharon was here again tonight. Honest, sincere, direct, genuine, he said to Estelle and me: "I came over especially to tell you that you simply must leave. There's a ship leaving tomorrow, the *Anna Maria*. Go, get out. You're leaving anyway on June 13th. So why not leave two weeks earlier?"

"We can't be packed by tomorrow."

"So leave unpacked. For the life of me I cannot understand this. You are putting your lives in danger. You have no right to stay. Suppose there is bombing, or shelling. Suppose there's hunger, and rationing, and standing in line for food."

(A ridiculous thought strikes me as he speaks. The prospect of

bombing and shelling, somehow, does not frighten me. But standing in line — this makes me panic. Why do I despise standing in
line so? There is something cow-ish about it: standing in line at the
trough doing nothing but waiting, waiting, waiting. And people in
lines in Israel are notoriously ill-mannered, always trying to push
ahead of you. This is the only country where the line forms from
the front.)

Aharon is probably right in everything he says. He made a
remark today which hit home: "Are you afraid of being called a
coward?" Certainly he has a point. But I have given up trying to
understand why we have chosen to stay. I only hope we don't regret
it. Or perhaps I should say, I hope to *live* to regret it. Right now, we'll
settle for life.

22 Iyar

Thursday, June 1

I DROVE INTO TEL AVIV today through Dizengoff Circle. Dizengoff has always repelled me because of its huge crowds, the packed sidewalk cafes, the impossible traffic, but mostly because of the hippies and beatniks that make the Circle their headquarters. I like beatnik types — but not in Israel. Somehow the Israeli beatnik tries too hard, and on him it just seems like bad make-up. I expect — certainly this is unfair of me — I expect a Jew, an Israeli, a member of a holy people, to be more than just an imitator of the latest fashion, sloppy or otherwise. Somehow it all seems unnatural and phony when out of the mouth comes Hebrew.

But today, Dizengoff Circle was quiet. No crowds, plenty of room at the sidewalk cafes, no traffic. It was almost bucolic, rustic, rural. But as much as I love things bucolic, rustic, and rural, I think I would have hugged and kissed them if I could have only seen a couple of beatniks.

As depressing as Dizengoff was, Tel Aviv in general was good for the morale. The people seem fairly cheerful today, and the grimness is below the surface. I suppose it is primarily in the smaller towns where one really feels the impact of the crisis.

One poor woman in Tel Aviv experienced her own personal crisis today. It was late afternoon, and I walked over to the Great Synagogue on Allenby Street to daven *Minchah*. In the middle of the services a woman comes in and sits down in the rear, far away from the *minyan*, but not behind the *mechitzah*. The *gabbai* approaches her with great dignity and proclaims in stentorian tones: "My dear woman, you must get on the other side of the *mechitzah*. This is not Haifa." I felt sorry for her. And for Haifa, which has over two hundred synagogues and many yeshivos. But its reputation is that of a port city and no one in Israel will admit that there is any kind of religious life in Haifa. Poor Haifa. Poor woman.

We learned today that President Aref of Iraq has dispatched his soldiers to Jordan. His orders are "to remove Israel from the map. With God's help we will meet in Tel Aviv and Haifa." Strange how everyone invokes God, for good and for evil.

Why am I keeping this journal?

A good question. I don't really know the answer. By now it has become an obsession with me. (The more I write the less answers I know to anything, it seems.) Is this for myself, so that in later years I can read it, and remember? Is it for posterity, so that if we are all blown up, someone may find this and know how it really was, unvarnished and unromanticized: that we were not heroes, and not cowards; that we were hopeful for peace, and did not want war; that we were afraid of bloodshed, of killing, but also familiar enough with it not to be paralyzed by the prospect; that we were hopeful that the great powers would help, but bitterly aware that they cared little about us; and that ultimately we knew that only one Great Power would help us.

Or am I writing this because it helps me keep my sanity?

Israelis are a very impatient people. They are highly intense, always in a hurry, very nervous, quite aggressive, quick to lose their tempers. This is not to say that Israelis are unkind. It is only that they are not given to the niceties of courtesy to which one is accustomed in the United States, particularly in the South.

Driving on the highways, for example, is nerve-shattering: everyone is in a feverish rush. Israeli friends to whom I point this out reply that Israel is a frontier country, that its people live under a constant state of siege, that they are beset by enemies on all sides, and that all this takes its toll on manners. Accepted. What is paradoxical and remarkable, however, is that during the past two weeks, when tension has been at its highest peak since 1948, there has been a noticeable increase in the amenities and civilities of ordinary life. Strangers say hello to one another; people seem to be more concerned about others' feelings.

In Itchkovitch this morning an old, white-bearded man came in during services carrying a heavy suitcase laden with books on Kabbalah. He was busily trying to sell them to the worshippers.

A man says to him, Kabbalah? For this you must have a mind.

Salesman: Nu, so who says you don't have a mind? You have a mind!

Customer: A mind! I left my mind with Hitler.

Salesman: Hitler? Hitler's a dead dog!

Customer: Yes, but he took my mind before he died. All he left me was my body.

In the evening, our neighbor Mrs. Ganon pays us a rare visit. She is twenty-two, Swiss, the mother of two.

"Well, I finally have my ticket. I am leaving."

"Oh. Well, good luck." To be perfectly honest, we are beginning to feel rather superior to those who are panicking, but we try not to show it.

"You mean you people are not leaving? But your Embassy says you must leave!" She is genuinely shocked. She had taken it for granted that all Americans are going. "Why are you not leaving? Are you not afraid?"

We are afraid to tell her that we are not yet fully afraid so we gently try to steer the conversation elsewhere. We are truly relieved when she finally goes.

But the truth is that we are becoming a kind of curiosity on the streets. Total strangers keep stopping us and saying, "How is it that you're not leaving?" They are genuinely pleased that we are still here. And just as genuinely surprised. But our responses have not jelled yet and we don't know quite what to say to them. Noble sentiments will sound hollow, as will patriotism, so we say things like, "I can't leave you behind to handle all this by yourself"; or "Everything will be fine, why should I leave?" Today we evolved the best reply, which we use only sparingly to certain kinds of people: "We don't have the courage to leave." This is very close to the truth.

All these questions have forced us to try to articulate to ourselves just why it is that we are staying, and we really do not know for certain. Firstly, our instincts say "don't leave." And most reasons, logical as they are, are only rational supports for what was an instinctive decision in the first place. All kinds of factors are involved: shame at leaving; desire not to give in to fear; a kind of bravado, maybe false; a wish to be a part of whatever will come; exhilaration at the crisis; the feeling that we are involved in historical events; the desire to share with the community of Israel whatever will come. If this were, say, France, we would never feel this way. I would get up and run — fast — and not look back. But this is not France.

That Liberian tanker has not been mentioned in the news since Monday. Today, however, there was word that she has been ordered by her owners to turn back and not to run the blockade. Too bad. One way or the other, the suspense would have been over.

All this is darkly humorous. For ten days, we have been hearing all kinds of pious pronouncements about an international fleet which would challenge the blockade. The United States evidently promised Eban that she would organize such a fleet. Now this powerful international armada has withered down into one insignificant, rumored, unconfirmed, unheard-from Liberian tanker — which has now turned back. Some armada.

23 Iyar

Friday, June 2

TODAY I ACHIEVED A pinnacle in my career. Now I have truly arrived. After returning from the swift completion of my appointed rounds, from which neither snow nor rain nor heat nor gloom of night nor Nasser stayed me, the post office *menahel* welcomed me with a broad smile, ushered me grandly into his office, waved me to a chair beside his desk, and offered me a hot glass of tea — with lemon and sugar. Tea inside the *menahel's* office: have I not arrived?

Yesterday evening I went into Carlebach's bookstore to pay something on the huge bill I have run up there recently while I was drowning my tension in wild book-buying. Normally, the tiny place is overflowing with customers and browsers, and Carlebach holds forth with amusing anecdotes of the great and near-great. He is

111

probably the most respected scribe in Israel today, a huge, jolly man, with a great, scraggly beard. He has a sardonic sense of humor, a fine gift of irony, and I think he attracts people to his place by force of personality alone. The shop itself is always in shambles, yet he knows the precise spot where any book can be found — usually on the floor in a forgotten corner.

Last night, Carlebach's was empty. He was sitting all alone there behind his table, the ubiquitous glass of tea untouched, a glazed look in his eyes as if he were viewing some far-away scene. Without looking at me he murmured in a monotone: "They just slaughtered us and killed us all out a few years ago. We who were left — human rags — came here. For a little peace, a little rest. What do they want from us? They are talking, talking, talking in the United Nations and having their cocktails in their lounges and making arrangements and deals. And the prospect of another two million Jews exterminated does not excite them in the least. I am not afraid of dying, of being killed, but the wrong of it all, the sheer injustice, the brutality of this world of ours. I am sick, I tell you. Sick at heart."

Despite Carlebach, the air of foreboding seems to have generally lifted today. It probably won't last, but it is pleasant to see a few smiles once again. Part of this is no doubt because of the news that the United States aircraft carrier Intrepid is scheduled to go through the Suez Canal today. Of course it is all part of the chess game with Russia. The Russians send their fleet through the Dardanelles towards the Mediterranean; the United States sends its ships towards Suez. There is nothing concrete in any of this, nothing on which to base any hopes, but how long can gloom last? Like a fog it has to lift — "and then moves on" — even if there is no apparent cause. And nothing has really changed fundamentally.

We do see a few more soldiers on the streets today, however.

Some of them have been sent home from the front for a brief furlough. They walk the streets in their battle dress, their huge automatic rifles slung over their shoulders. It is good to see them.

I am probably making a pest of myself, but I ask everyone what he thinks is going to happen. Interesting, the varying reactions of the different ethnic groups. The Polish and Hungarian Jews, who have gone through so much already in Europe, are very worried and shake their heads sadly. But the Yemenites to a man still have that peaceful and simple faith: whatever God says and does will be good.

I think about Rav Levenstein's *shmuess* last night about *pachad* — fear — and how it can make people leave everything behind, as it has done in Israel these past several weeks: "See how strong is *pachad*," he said. "People are ready to leave their most precious possessions and flee. Because of fear of injury, because of fear of death. Would that we had *pachad* like that about committing a sin…"

The live broadcasts from the desert with the singers and actors entertaining the troops continue to fascinate the country. There is a certain poignant wistfulness about them.

Telegrams and special delivery letters are still pouring in to American students from parents abroad. Leave now. Plane tickets are being sent. The yeshiva boys are on the horns of a dilemma: the obligation to obey parents, and the obligation to the Holy Land.

Eshkol's disastrous talk is still a popular topic. There is a great deal of conversation about Ben Gurion. If he were Prime Minister, it is said, we would have already reacted strongly instead of just waiting for diplomatic miracles. Similarly, they are saying, if Kennedy were the American President he would not be afraid. He was strong, he had courage. He would clearly tell the Russians to pull out.

I cannot agree with either might-have-been. Firstly, we have to deal with what *is*, and not with what we would like the *is* to be. In addition, the patience which Eshkol is now showing may be a sign of strength, and might ultimately redound to Israel's benefit if military action has to be taken later: We waited for the great powers to act, they procrastinated, we were being strangled, we acted. Nor can I agree about LBJ and JFK. Because Kennedy was young and vigorous, people assume that he would have done things differently. He undoubtedly would have behaved in the same studiously calm and restrained manner that LBJ is displaying.

Nevertheless, there is a deep resentment against the whole world — including the democracies, and especially England and the United States, who seem to be changing their tune every other day. In the meantime, the Israeli economy is the great sufferer. The recession was bad enough before. It is now absolutely impossible. This fact, plus Israel's pride, will ultimately force Israel to clear Tiran somehow. But even then, there remains the open Egyptian border, the danger of infiltrators, terrorism, sabotage. And unless something is done, Eshkol will fall and Ben Gurion or Dayan or someone more militant will come in. The options open to Israel are very few.

24 Iyar

Shabbos, June 3

I T HAS BEEN THE most relaxing Shabbos in three weeks, very little tension in the air, and Rechov Akiva was again crowded with promenaders. There were not many younger men on the streets but there were a number of soldiers with their families. It was an odd juxtaposition: the women and children in their Shabbos finery; and the soldiers, many with beards and *peyos*, wearing their camouflage tan, yellow, and green fatigues.

The feeling of relief which has swept across the country is due partially to the conviction that the crisis has played itself out — and especially to Moshe Dayan's sudden elevation to Defense Minister. At his news conference yesterday he was quite relaxed, even witty and bright. Wit and brightness are something this country has sorely lacked these past few weeks. Our leadership has been dull and prosaic, and whether or not you like

Dayan — and not everyone likes him — he is anything but dull.

On everyone's lips tonight is his quip that it is both too late and too early: too late to react to Nasser militarily, since the element of surprise is gone; too early to say that all diplomatic means have been exhausted. Obviously, then, Dayan is saying that we are in for a long period of waiting. So we will wait. How does the old saying go? *"A Yid hat tzeit* — A Jew has time."

Last night the whole family and I went to daven at Vizhnitz. We walked through open, moonlit fields, the Shabbos songs wafting from houses here and there, up winding streets filled with strolling couples, and climbed a steep hill to the central building which is a combination shul, school, dining room, and *beis midrash.*

Vizhnitz is a town in Romania, beloved by Jews because of its famous Chassidic dynasty and the great Rebbe of Vizhnitz. After the European holocaust, the shattered remnants of the Vizhnitz Jews found their way to Israel together with their beloved Rebbe, and there they took up once again exactly what they had always been doing.

Geographically within Bnei Brak, the Vizhnitz area is a separate entity, almost a ghetto within a ghetto. They have their own pre-schools and schools and seminaries, their own butchers and bakers, shuls, hotel, apartment buildings, cemetery. They have succeeded in transplanting everything from Europe. Even their shul is a replica of the one they had in Romania.

On Friday nights, the men of Vizhnitz dress up in their *shtreim-lach, bekeshes,* and white, knee-length stockings into which they tuck their trousers, and go to pray with the Rebbe in the large study-hall. The praying is ecstatic and joyous, filled with hand-clapping, singing, and dancing. During davening the Chassidim, hundreds of men with their children, form a large circle around the Rebbe and dance vigorously as they sing the haunting, plaintive melodies with which they usher in Shabbos. Even a stranger to Vizhnitz is carried away by the electric presence of the gentle, white-bearded Rebbe and his hand-clapping Chassidim. The crisis was millions of miles away from Vizhnitz.

How these pious Jews in Israel can pray: Ponevezh with its energizing passion, Vizhnitz with its liberating emotion. This is unvarnished worship, without ostentation and glitter: honest and simple and true worship.

After davening everyone goes home to partake of the Shabbos meal with his own family. At ten in the evening they return to the *beis midrash* and wait anxiously for the Rebbe to arrive and begin his regular Friday night *tisch*.

The Rebbe appears at the door. An explosion of sound and movement. The Chassidim sing and clap and dance around him. Majestically he enters the room in his resplendent silk *bekeshe*, blue robe, *shtreimel*, supported on his right hand by his son and on his left by his son-in-law. Is it my imagination or is he floating in? They crowd around him and fairly carry him to his chair at the head of the long table. He sits at a dais, surrounded on all sides by young children in their own *bekeshes* and black hats. Around the table special bleachers — literally — have been erected so that all can see the Rebbe. They follow his every move, his every look, his every gesture. His face is ruddy and has an unnatural, unwordly glow. His son is seated at his right hand, his son-in-law at his left. The Rebbe sings the beginning of *Shalom Aleichem*, and the hall resounds with a chorus. He sings one stanza, they respond. More *zemiros* follow. The young Chassidim sway rhythmically to and fro, eyes rooted to the Rebbe. He breaks bread. The pieces are distributed to the elders at the table, who take a piece and then pass it along to the youngsters. By the time it reaches me in the rear bleachers it is a crumb. The child next to me breaks off a speck, puts it to his mouth and passes the rest, a tiny atom, a molecule, to his neighbor, who devours it hungrily. The hall is packed, but more people crowd in. In America this crush would take place only for a movie star, an athlete, a famous politician who passes through town on a rare occasion. Here it is done every single week. The Vizhnitzer Rebbe is a holy man, and the Chassidim believe in his special powers and repeat fantastic stories and legends about him.

He begins to eat fish and *challah*. Slowly he breaks the fish with his fork, carefully lifts it to his mouth, methodically chews it, swallows, and dabs his lips carefully with a napkin. His son, himself a long-bearded man of fifty and a noted scholar, gently brushes the bread crumbs from his father's beard.

I am standing in the rear on my tiptoes, straining to see. Some of the Chassidim notice this and make space for me to get in closer. I am obviously a stranger, and they are genuinely pleased to have me among them. Hands stretch forth in *shalom aleichem*s to me, they smile frequently, they ask me to join in a dance. Israelis in general are very reserved with strangers, but not so the Vizhnitzer Chassidim who go out of their way to put me at ease.

Near me, two young boys of twelve or thirteen are conversing in Yiddish.

One says, "Vizhnitz is not what it used to be. Now it is too much like the Gerrer Chassidim. Whoever heard of anyone ever sleeping at the Rebbe's Friday night *tisch?* Look at that Chassid over there — sound asleep. And look at the one next to him — same thing. That never used to happen here at Vizhnitz."

The other young Chassid puts his fingers in his ears and runs away, shouting, "I will not listen to this kind of talk about Vizhnitz."

Later, when I met Estelle outside, she had tears in her eyes. "Really," she said, "could God allow such people to be destroyed?"

I do not think so. But someone ought to inform Iraqi President Aref that he doesn't have a chance with God. The Vizhnitzers surely have first call on Him.

In all the shuls today there appeared printed leaflets in the form of a letter written by Rav Shmuel Halevi Wosner, generally acknowledged as one of the leading rabbis and scholars in Israel. Rav Wosner is a young man as scholars go — probably in his late forties. He is a handsome man, with coal eyes, a rich black beard, tall and ascetic and fiery.

The salutation of the letter is striking. Following the traditional formula, he cites the Torah portion of the week, *Bemidbar*, which is part of a phrase in the first verse: *Bemidbar Sinai* — literally, "in the Sinai Desert." This is in itself timely enough. But then Rav Wosner adds, "*Gematria beshalom* — Whose numerical equivalent equals 'in peace.'" Every Hebrew letter has a numerical value: *alef* equals one, *beis* equals two, *gimmel* equals three, and so on. Following this method, the numerical value of the Hebrew for "in the Sinai Desert" is 378. And the numerical value of "in peace" is also 378. The Sinai Desert, therefore, equals "in peace." Wonderful. May it be so.

But the letter itself: it is actually a mosaic of Torah references and allusions. Across the top is the salutation in capital letters:

TO MY BROTHERS AND MY FRIENDS AND OUR DEAR STUDENTS WHO DWELL IN OUR HOLY LAND.

> This is a time of tribulation for Yaakov. Our Holy Torah has assured us, "The sword shall not pass through your land," and now that our enemies have lifted up their head and said, "Let

us go and destroy them" (God forbid), we must understand that good and evil come not from God but are rather caused by our own deeds, for "what does Hashem require of you but to fear Him."

The Rambam has written: It is a positive commandment to cry out and to sound the shofar whenever a tribulation occurs, so that everyone will understand that because of evil deeds has this befallen them, as is written, "Your sins have withheld the good from you." And this will remove the tribulation from them. However, if they do not cry out and do not shout to God, but instead say, "This thing has befallen us as part of the normal ways of the world, and this tribulation is merely an accidental and purposeless event," this is an evil way and causes them to cleave even more to their evil deeds, and the present tribulation will increase to additional tribulations. That is what the Torah means, "And you have walked with Me in evil (keri)"; that is, I will bring upon you tribulations so that you shall repent. If you will say that it is keri — which means "accident" — I will add to your tribulations with greater wrath.

Therefore, it is necessary first and foremost to pour out our hearts like water to Him, and to increase prayer and worship to The Awesome One…

But let no man say that it is enough to pray. For repentance is not a matter of words but of deeds — and the primary duty of a man should be to return anything which may be ill-gotten, whether it be through theft or interest or usury or the like.

- To increase our study of Torah, the Torah of truth, in order to be able to practice it.
- To study the *Code of Law* for daily life, for this is truly life-giving….

It is impossible to detail all the things a man should begin to do. Each man knows the secret recesses of his own heart, and in his own way let each man regret his sins and weep for the Shechinah — the presence of God — which is in exile...

As for our brethren, the children of Israel, who are on the seas, on the land, in the deserts, and in all places of danger, may the Holy One protect them from all trials and tribulations, and may He have pity on His people Israel... and may we be worthy of knowing that the Kingdom is Hashem's and He is the ruler of the nations. And let us reject the false notion of "my might and my power," and then will Hashem take pity upon us.

And may the Holy One in His great goodness and compassion have mercy on our holy land, and let not innocent blood be spilled upon it. May the passage "And I will grant peace to the land" be fulfilled; and let us be worthy of walking in His statutes as our righteous Mashiach approaches in infinite mercy. Amen.

The crowds read the letter quietly and solemnly. It is deeply moving.

A second leaflet also appeared today, this one from Rav Ashlag, the great teacher of Kabbalah and mysticism. It is entitled: A SECTION OF THE *ZOHAR* THAT CASTS LIGHT ON OUR CURRENT SITUATION. The notice consists simply of a quotation from the *Zohar*, a source book of the Kabbalah. Based on *Devarim* 28, which contains the long section of curses which may someday befall Israel (and which, dear God, dear God, have already been fulfilled a thousand times over), the *Zohar* says: "God has already sworn that he will never destroy Israel." There is a particularly remarkable comment on verse 68 of that chapter: "And Hashem will bring you back to Egypt in ships." Says the *Zohar*: "This means that it will come to pass that all the inhabitants of the world will descend upon Israel in their ships, and they will attempt to erase Israel from the world.

And all of them will sink into the depths of the ocean as happened in the days of yore."

But our eyes and hearts were fastened on the *Zohar*'s comment on the last half of verse 68: "And there will you offer yourselves for sale unto your enemies as slaves, without anyone to buy you." *Zohar*:

> After all the people of the world will have gathered against Israel, Israel will think that she is destroyed and that she will be sold to her enemies as slaves as it is written, "And there will you offer yourselves for sale as slaves." It is not written, "You will be sold," but "You will offer yourselves for sale"; that is, you will think that you are going to be sold. This is not so, for it is also written, "Without anyone to buy you": this means, no one will be able to dominate you.

The *Zohar* continues:

> All this will occur at the end of days. Everything depends on the return to God. And everything is hidden. As it is written (*Devarim* 29:8), "That you may grow wise in all that you do": he who has a heart will look, and he will know that he must return to his Master.
>
> Eliyahu the prophet said: Look carefully. In the most terrible section of the curses, there is revealed the nature of Israel's redemption.

One thing is certain: the religious leadership of Israel has truly risen to the occasion, much more so than has the political leadership. The rabbis are alive to the implications of these days. Their religious sensitivities are heightened by their training, and they do not merely pray, but attempt to learn and understand and apprehend what it is that Hashem requires of them — of us — in this hour.

The basic point of Judaism's belief in God is that nothing happens by accident. The Jew must always be exquisitely and painfully aware of himself and his relationship to God at any given moment. He is not to accept adversity dumbly, nor is he to rebel blindly. He is to ask, faithfully, "Why has this befallen me, and what can I do to rectify it?"

25 Iyar

Sunday, June 4

THE FEELING IS UNIVERSAL here that we are in for a long period of waiting and that in some unknown way the dust will settle peacefully. But we are taking no chances. We are still reciting *Tehillim* 83 and 142 after every morning and evening worship.

There is a beautiful story making the rounds these days. A foreign correspondent is talking to a rabbi in Jerusalem and asks him how he thinks the crisis will be finally settled.

"By one of two ways," the rabbi replies. "By a miracle or by a natural way."

The correspondent asks, "What would be the natural way?"

"To settle it by a miracle," answers the rabbi.

"And what would be the miracle?"

"To settle it in a natural way," says the rabbi.

125

In an Orthodox enclave like Bnei Brak the obvious reaction to any crisis is a new turning to God and prayer and Torah study. Even without the religious spurring on by the rabbis, the pious Jews would have naturally turned to these matters.

The normally non-Orthodox Jews, however, find themselves in an anomalous position. They are rather self-conscious about using the name of God, they feel it is a kind of anachronism for them and are a bit embarrassed about it. And yet these are critical times, and for any Jew, who is at most one generation removed from a pious parent or grandparent, not to invoke the name of God is almost unnatural. Haltingly, in a kind of spiritual stammer, but nevertheless steadily, the people here are resurrecting their dormant religious consciousness.

Just today, for example, a hitchhiker I picked up declared quite gratuitously that he was not religious, "But I do believe in God, and I know that this is His land, so I am not really worried."

"All that sounds pretty religious to me," I replied.

"Well, I do not pray, I do not keep the commandments. But we are an old people, we have an ancient culture, and this land — I want no other place and I will die to stay in this place. But I will not have to die, because God wants us to live, I am sure."

He does not pray, he says, so he does not know that his sentiment is echoed in *Tehillim* 20 which is part of the daily prayers: "Some trust in chariots, some in horses; but we call upon the name of Hashem, our God."

Today I ran into Rabbi Shlomo Lorincz, member of the Knesset who represents the religious parties. "Well, what will be?" I said. "Shall we leave or shall we stay? We are scheduled to leave on June 13. Do you think we will make it?"

"To me," he says with a smile, "it looks good. Do not leave now, there is no need to panic. Everything will work out and you will be able to leave just as you planned."

His words are said with such quiet confidence and assurance that it underscores my feeling of relief and relaxation. If anyone should know, Lorincz should.

What is most interesting about all the God-invoking among the religious Jews is that they are not using religion or God as a guarantee for the destruction of their enemies. Instead, they are looking at themselves, at their own shortcomings, and working very hard at spiritual self-improvement. There is a marked increase, for example, in the giving of charity.

Contrast this with the Arabs. Pardon the pun, but my God! Radio Cairo is filled with Allah who will lead the Arab peoples into battle to annihilate every man, woman, and child in Israel, etc., etc., etc.

26 Iyar

Monday, June 5

THERE IS A RELAXED feeling in the air at *Shacharis* this morning. Everyone now knows that everything will be all right. We have evolved good reasons, too. Nasser does not want war; his best troops are involved in Aden; he has over-extended himself; the Great Powers do not want war; Hussein won't fight; the Arabs will quarrel among themselves; every day that passes is in our favor. And during the night we heard that Nasser has dispatched his Vice President to Washington for talks. "Hah!" snorts Bonner after davening. "He's desperate, and now he's going to ask Johnson to get him off the hook."

Funny how your mood dictates your thinking. Just a few days ago we were saying that every day that passes is in their favor, that when it comes to Israel the Arabs *are* united. But then we were in a black mood.

Back in our apartment. The children are gulping down breakfast, and I get ready to go to the university. At ten to eight we hear the throaty sound of wailing sirens. We run to the window. Everyone else is at his window, too. We look down at the street below. Traffic is moving, children are walking to school, women are carrying groceries. Everything is quite normal. But the siren does not stop. I snap on the radio. No news. Only the usual silly morning music.

Estelle asks a neighbor, "What is it?"

"*Mekulkal*, broken. Something must be wrong with the air-raid alarm system."

I go downstairs. I meet Sheinfeld. He is on his way to Tel Aviv.

"What is it?" I ask.

"It's a drill. Just a drill. Nothing to worry about." And he disappears around the corner.

I look up at the sky. It is too blue for anything serious to be afoot. Under such a sky only peace can reign. The sirens have stopped. I return to the apartment. Estelle wonders if we should send the children to school today. I suggest that we send only the two older children and keep the two younger ones at home just in case. It is now eight-twenty. In the excitement I have missed the eight o'clock news. A long loud siren begins, not a wail this time, but an endless monotone. The all-clear.

I go down to the car. I have to make a stop at the bank before I go on to the lecture. Bura is walking down the street. He smiles.

"It has begun," he says cheerfully.

"What has begun?"

"Fighting. They are fighting."

"Where?"

"In the Negev."

"How do you know?" I ask. "Is it just another rumor?"

"No, no. No rumor. I just heard it on the radio."

Estelle is on the porch upstairs. I relay the news to her: "They are fighting in the Negev!"

"Really?"

"Really. It's probably only a little skirmish. I'm going. See you later."

On the way to the bank I turn on the car radio. I catch the eight-thirty news: "*Dover Tzahal modia* — The army spokesman has announced that in response to an Egyptian attack our forces have replied and several tank and air battles are taking place."

Well, I say to myself, it won't last for more than an hour. Just a skirmish.

In the bank, I mention it to the teller. He looks up from his book. "Really?"

"Really."

He continues working without a sound.

I go on to the university. In the campus parking lot there are four army trucks, covered by camouflage netting. One of the drivers tells me that they are taking over the dormitories for the wounded.

Clusters of students are standing here and there listening to the nine o'clock news. I recognize the calm voice of Emek Peri. No one speaks.

I dutifully go to my regular lecture hall. Two of my students — girls — are already there, waiting for me. Rachel — who takes a two-hour train ride from Haifa every Monday morning to be here — asks me if I will excuse her today; she has volunteered for hospital work. Dorit asks permission to go home, she is frightened. I am left alone, feeling completely helpless and useless.

Perhaps I will go over to the post office and help them out, although they are not expecting me today.

On the way out, I stop at the administration building. Professor Yammon is just entering the building as I walk in. He sees me and says in his British-accented Hebrew, "*Kol hakavod* to you, you stayed behind to be with us." And he breezes past me to the chairman of the Humanities Division, looks at his watch, and says cheerfully, "I say, weren't we supposed to meet at nine?"

"Yes, that's right," says the chairman, also British. And, not to be outdone, he adds a smile.

"Well," says Yammon, "we're late." And off they go, arm in arm. You have to give them credit, these British, with their upper lips so typically stiff.

Isn't it remarkable how Jews, who are a very distinct and unique ethnic group, so easily take on the characteristics and coloration of the culture in which they happen to live at any given moment in history? British Jews are Jews, but so British; German Jews are Jews — ask Hitler — but so German. And American Jews, and Dutch Jews: unmistakably Jews, and at the same time unmistakably an integral part of their countries and cultures. Of course, this is true of all minority groups in a way, with one major qualification. Other minority groups, after a generation or two, lose all traces of their origins. Jews so far have been able to maintain them.

Inside, the secretary is just finishing her conversation on the telephone as I walk in. She blurts out quietly, "I am going home. My husband just called, he works at Lod Airport — they have closed it down. He wants me to go home immediately. He says it is very serious. Very heavy fighting."

The siren comes on again, soft and whispering at first and then a loud, deep-throated scream. Almost immediately the all-clear sounds, a long, brooding moan.

If this is the real thing I had better be home with the family, and I jump into the car and drive off. On the way home, a new air-raid alarm, first over the radio and then outside. I am on the open highway, there is no safe spot on which to pull over and park, so I speed up and roar into Bnei Brak at eighty miles an hour. This time the town is deserted. No one is on the streets, shops are closed. The siren is still screeching insistently. I dash upstairs to our apartment. No sound. I look into all the rooms. Empty. Where is everyone? Then I remember. In the shelter. I jump downstairs. The shelter is long and narrow and dark. Rickety folding chairs and a few cots line the bare, concrete walls. Estelle and Chavah and Amram and dozens of our neighbors are all sitting there clutching their little bags of food.

"Some skirmish," Estelle says with a smile.

In twenty minutes the all-clear sounds again. We go up to the apartment and turn on the radio. Martial music. Old familiar marches. I must say that even martial music is a relief compared to the usual morning fare on Kol Yisrael Radio. Neighbor Ganon comes in.

"This is war," he says. "There is no question now. During Suez in '56 they also began the day by playing martial music."

The music stops and a voice comes on. It is a quiet and solemn voice, addressing itself to *"Chayalei Tzahal,* soldiers of the armed forces." The voice — I recognize it now: it is Dayan — states that we are engaged in air battles with the enemy and that our tanks and our ground forces are moving to repel the attack. "We will defend our land against all our enemies, although we are a small people, outnumbered and surrounded." We are not interested in territorial conquests, he says, but in peace. But we will fight in order to live, and we will be victorious. He wishes them well, and concludes: "Soldiers of Israel, in you today lies our hope and our trust."

There follows a call-up of reserves, to "appear immediately at previously arranged checkpoints, according to the following code name of your unit." Twenty-two code names are then listed by the announcer. Even in the midst of all the excitement, they are fascinating: Lovers of Zion, Nice Shave, The Rock and the Wave, Womb Companion, The Open Window, My Faithful Friend, Born in the Land, Wedding March, Golden Paper, Past and Future, Rest Corner, Peace and Blessing.

Some skirmish.

Estelle finally speaks the unspoken thoughts of both of us: "Well, this is it. We chose to be here, and we're here."

I do not answer.

The radio is now giving detailed instructions about air-raid procedures and tonight's blackout. I know it is madness, but I turn on the tape recorder and place it at the radio. Some day we may want to listen to the whole thing at our leisure.

Air-raid sirens begin to plead again. We grab our packages of food and water — and transistor radio — and run down to the shelter. Everyone is very pleasant and cordial and cooperative. The children — there are now about thirty of them — are surprisingly well-behaved and disciplined.

We hear thudding noises in the distance. Bombs? Cannons? Artillery? Shells? No one knows. Listen. A new sound now — staccato — the sound of anti-aircraft guns. No wonder they are called ack-ack guns. Exactly. *Ack-ack-ack, ack-ack-ack-ack*. There are other sounds: *poom — poom poom poom poom*, stopping suddenly like interrupted sentences. The ground trembles beneath us. Are they bombing Tel Aviv? Everyone is silent, listening intently. If the children are frightened they hide it well. But they are frightened. Amram's eyes are huge black marbles, and Chavah is staring at me.

The children! It hits us suddenly that Ilan and Jonathan are still at school. Do they have a shelter at school?

"Yes, yes," say the neighbors, "don't worry, a fine shelter."

Good. They have a fine shelter at school. Odd how grateful one can be for a simple thing like a fine shelter at school. Nice project for the next PTA meeting. Furnish the fine shelter at school. Wall-to-wall carpeting, wall-to-wall everything. Wall-to-wall children. They have a fine shelter at school. Oh, how lovely how sweet how nice how pleasant how comforting to know that they have a fine shelter at school and the air battles are going on above us and tank battles and infantry and *poom poom poom* as the ground trembles and they have a fine fine fine shelter at school don't worry yes a fine shelter at school.

Good Lord, our Father, our King save us for Your sake Hashem is my shepherd I shall not want the dead cannot praise Hashem some trust in chariots and some in horses but we call upon the name of Hashem our God blessed are You O God redeemer of Israel and Creator of fine shelters at school.

The all-clear sounds. I dash out of the shelter and run the two blocks to the school to pick up the boys. By the time I get there, all the children are out in the school yard. Ilan and Jonathan and their classmates are gathered around their teacher, a man of sixty. He is gently telling them not to be afraid, for God will not permit His holy land to be destroyed. I take the boys and we run back to the shelter.

It is excruciating. The radio gives us absolutely no news. It is now almost noon. We have been in and out of the shelter all morning. The booming echo of artillery and/or shelling is heard. There is a war on, but where are we fighting? In the desert? In the North? And how are we doing? Maybe the enemy is advancing on us.

Unlikely, but anything is possible. In the back of my mind — and I keep it to myself — is the terrible, lurking fear of Egyptian missiles. There is no defense against missiles directed against civilian centers. But all we hear are the brief, curt, quiet announcements that "we are engaging the enemy on all fronts." And martial music. And replays of Dayan's charge to the troops. And a pep talk by General Rabin. And the various unit code names, repeated every fifteen minutes, and instructions about what to do. And martial music.

In desperation we turn the dial to Radio Cairo. They are playing the same martial music! So is Radio Amman, and Radio Damascus. The Arabic announcers are hysterical. They scream and harangue and I recognize the words Israel and Palestine every few sentences. I must admit, however, that they are a welcome respite from the cool matter-of-fact tones of my beloved Emek Peri. At least they show some emotion. Oh, how cool, how collected, how very, very self-consciously Western these Israelis have become.

Kol Yisrael Radio has apparently run out of marches and is now repeating the same ones every so often. The River Kwai march — what is its name? The March of Colonel something-or-other — seems to be the favorite. It is ludicrous, but every time they play it I can think of nothing but Alec Guinness.

During the next all-clear I notice Bura running down the street toward his house. Maybe he has some news. I call to him. He is smiling as always but this time it is a little sheepish: "I knew there would be a war, but I didn't think there would be any air-raids. I'm really sorry about it." And he hurries off.

Finally, at two o'clock — we are back in the shelter — as if it had been uncorked from a full bottle, we get a flood of hard news. At 1:20, Kfar Saba was shelled by Jordanian artillery; since this morning, Jordanian artillery has been pounding Jerusalem, and at 1:35 twelve civilians were wounded in the center of Jerusalem; at 1:50, Lachish in the north was shelled by artillery, as was the Mei Ami settlement; Syrian planes have penetrated Israeli air space and bombed Netanya (ten miles north of us) and Megiddo in the Galilee; Egyptian artillery has attacked Nahal Oz in the Negev.

The news is over. And now that we have heard it we wish we hadn't. There is an ominous ring to it. And Jordan — sly, treacherous Jordan — is in it too, up to her neck. A voice from the far corner of the shelter: "What are our troops doing? Why no news about what we are doing? Surely we're not just sitting still, are we?"

"From all sides, from all sides," Mrs. Herman says with a nod of her head.

"*Hayardeinim* — The Jordanians. They're in it, too. This is worse than Suez. Then we had only to worry about the Egyptians."

"*Yihyeh tov* — It will be good."

But we are worried and apprehensive. And the sirens wail us in and out of the shelter regularly. We run down dutifully, we trudge back up. Gradually, the shelter fills up with people and with furniture: mattresses, cribs, pillows, jugs of water, buckets of sand. Some families make plans to spend the night. Chavah begs permission of us to spend the night in the shelter with her friends.

It is late afternoon, the sun is setting far out over the Mediterranean, and still we have no news about our own troops. Does anyone have any news? Nothing, only the droning repetition of Jordanian shelling and Syrian bombardment. Nothing, only those terrifying alarms, an exact, mechanical duplication of the human cry — like an infant's sobbing. Shall I get maudlin and say that it is symbolic of a mankind which is still in its infancy and has to fight wars?

The lack of regular news is particularly hard on Americans, accustomed as we are to full and detailed news reports every hour on the hour. So what do we do? We ask total strangers, What's new? And if there is nothing new we exchange some theories, or create some rumors or likely facts. In a time like this, everyone leans on everyone else. Nothing brings people together like danger shared. The same was true on the ship coming over: people who a day earlier ignored one another became friendly as soon as the ocean got rough and things started tossing around. Today in Israel you can stop a total stranger on the street and get a good conversation.

But what is most exhilarating about a war, so fresh and so cleansing, is that one's own personality and one's own self and one's own problems and unhappinesses and bitternesses and frustrations all seem to fade away into nothingness. Nothing matters but the common good, the common safety, the common victory. And since everyone is equally in peril everyone is suddenly quite equal.

But somewhere, in the midst of all this exhilaration, someone is bleeding and someone is dying and somewhere a mother or a wife is opening a telegram in dread, and this thought serves to remove any illusions about the glories and grandeurs of war. It is only in a society where human life means nothing that war can be grand and cleansing. But where is there such a society? In China, do not mothers weep? In Russia, do not wives grieve? In Nazi Germany did not tears fall for the fallen? And if a cannibal in darkest Africa is slain by the poison spear of an enemy tribesman, do not his own tribe and his own mate and his own child mourn for him? What kind of senseless talk is this about war being exhilarating and fresh and cleansing?

Today the greetings to me have changed. No one asks, Why are you

```

staying? This is a moot question now, since all airports and harbors are closed and no one can get out if he wants to. Today the greeting is: "Ah, I see you stayed," with a smile of pleasure. It makes them feel good. It makes us feel good. No more fancy metaphysical reasons for staying. Perhaps the real reason was that we were certain there would be no shooting. We were quite wrong.

On R. Akiva Street I run into B., the well-known black-market dealer. For some reason, I am very fond of him.

"It will be all right. We will win," he says. Not very original, but hopeful. Then he looks around him and whispers to me, "I have vowed not to deal in 'black' until the war is over. The government needs the dollars." He is obviously very proud of his gesture. But it worries me: if B. has suddenly become patriotic, things must be very bad.

In all the excitement I have forgotten about my own brother Aharon. I jump into the car and dash over to his house. Things *are* serious. First of all, Aharon is not studying, and this fact alone is a sign of an emergency: in normal times, with six children underfoot, he stays immersed in his holy books from twelve to fifteen hours a day. But today he is putting up sandbags. And secondly, the woman on the third floor is not beating out her rugs. She is the one who, like so many Israelis, gives her rugs a daily thrashing over the porch railing. Naturally, the dust and dirt settle all over the porches below. Everyone used to suffer in silence. Rug-beating, after all, is a national sport in Israel. But when she began pouring buckets of water onto the neighbors' porches, they made bold to complain. Her reply deserves immortality: "What, do you think it's easy to live on the third floor?" This became an in-joke with Aharon and me. But today
```

she is not there in her customary batting position. Who knows, she might have dragged her beloved rugs down into the shelter with her.

"Well, Feldman," Aharon says to me. "This is it."

I am too embarrassed to say anything. For two weeks he has been hounding me to leave, and we wouldn't listen. But he is kind and does not bring up the subject.

"Well," I say finally, "it looks like you were right. I may have to stand in line after all."

"Very funny. Stop talking so much and grab a sandbag."

During a lull in the shelling, Ephraim comes over to the house. He is an American college student now studying at Ponevezh Yeshiva and has been very close to us. "I wanted to say goodbye to you," he says.

"Goodbye? Where are you going?"

"I'm not going, I'm staying here. But I just thought, just in case anything happens, you know — I just wanted to come by and…" His voice trails off.

I am somewhat embarrassed. "Well," I say lamely, "it will turn out all right. How are things going at the Yeshiva?"

"Everyone is down in the shelter, and we are all studying down there. The Rosh Yeshiva has put us on a kind of twenty-four hour duty for the duration. He wants at least fifty boys studying at every minute of the day and night. You know Rav Kahaneman. He says that Torah study is the generator which will keep our men in the field going."

Ephraim's visit touches me in an odd way. He is not frightened at all, he has had several opportunities to go back to the United States during the past two weeks but elected to stay. He only wants to be

140

sure to do what is right "just in case." I remember just then — and it is not a coincidence — that we owe money to the grocer and the butcher. Not much, but just in case, I had better pay all my debts. The grocery is locked — but I find the butcher shop open.

"Ah, *Adon* Feldman," he protests with a smile and the wave of a hand, "I trust you. Why do you have to come out in the middle of all this? You are leaving?"

"No, I am not leaving. I just thought, you know, just in case."

He thinks for a moment. "I will take the money, fine," he says. "You owe me forty-one lirot. I will take forty. You will owe me one lira. You will come in next week — there is no hurry — and you will pay me the one lira. I want you to owe me something. You understand."

"I understand."

Jerusalem is evidently being shelled very heavily. There are reports of many killed and wounded. I hope we now go into the Old City and take it once and for all. Wouldn't it be a fitting climax to our year to visit the Wailing Wall?

The afternoon lull ends abruptly at about four o'clock with the familiar wail. This time the shelter is packed. All the men who were caught at work since early morning have managed to get home. We begin setting up sleeping arrangements for the night. Sheinfeld balks: "No need to worry about tonight. The Arab pilots are afraid of night flying. You will sleep in your own beds tonight, mark my word." He is serious, but we laugh and continue arranging the cots and blankets and mattresses.

Sheinfeld is wrong: the worst and longest alert begins at night, at eight, and lasts for three hours. We can hear and see shells and/or bombs exploding in all directions as huge pillars of flame slash the darkness and disappear. Suddenly I am eight years old again, and my father has bought me a whole box of Fourth of July flares which I light up and wave and then toss up into the darkness and watch in awe as they flash and flicker and sputter into nothingness.

We hear the sound of airplanes overhead — ours or theirs? Flares shoot up, darkness becomes light for a full sixty seconds, *ack-ack* and *poom-poom-poom* punctuate the noise from a distance. It is like a stage set, pretty but unreal: the sudden bright orange, the yellow flares in the night sky, the crimson spew of flames bursting and flashing for a quick moment into the dark blue of the night. We huddle in the black shelter and we can only watch, and wonder, and hope.

I think suddenly of those who have fled back to the United States during these past weeks, and I wonder how they feel now. Safe and smug and secure, or stricken with terrible feelings of unease and guilt? Right now I can only feel sorry for them for having left Israel at such a time. No, more than just sorry. For the first time I feel something akin to contempt for them. It was, in the final analysis, a selfish act on their part. I never thought that in a dark, dank, damp shelter, in the midst of exploding shells, I could feel so smug and superior.

Everyone is in the shelter now except for Mrs. Tzvika and Mr. Katzenelenbogen. Mrs. Tzvika has not entered the shelter all day, and even now during the bombardment she sits, hunched, out on the steps, staring into the darkness, talking to no one. On her arm are the mute, tattooed numbers of the concentration camps. What is she thinking? About Dachau? About her husband, who was just called up last week? About her three young children?

Old Mr. Katzenelenbogen is not so mysterious about his refusal to enter the shelter. He has remained in his apartment all day. When I urge him to come down, he announces to me in his deep, booming voice, "I have lived in Israel for fifty years. I never hid from the Arabs, not in the 1930s, and not in 1948, and not in 1956. And I am not going to begin hiding now. I am too old to start crawling like a rat into a dark hole."

Mr. Herman and I step out of the shelter for a few minutes to get some fresh air, and we stare into the night. He murmurs in Yiddish: "A world, a world, an evil world. We have built up such a nice little country (*klein lendelle* was the phrase he used) so well organized, so well-managed, so nicely arranged, with parks and schools and highways — what other country has done so well in nineteen years? And now they want to destroy it all." He pauses and his eyes glisten. Suddenly he turns to me with a smile. "Well, my friend, now when you go back to America, you'll be able to tell them something about your experience. Now you'll be the life of the party."

I reply jokingly: "Listen, I didn't stay to be the life of the party, or to tell my experiences, or to sit in a dirty shelter with you. I stayed for one reason. I want to daven at the *Kotel Hamaaravi*." We laugh together.

It is deathly quiet for a while. Suddenly, behind us in the darkness, we hear a stirring in the bushes. We both jump — and then we realize that it is only the wind rustling through the branches. Mr. Herman sighs.

"*The sound of a driven leaf shall chase them,*" he says, quoting *Vayikra* 26:36. "This is what we have finally come to. Frightened at nothing."

Inside, the children are restless, trying bravely not to show their fear. Only children and fools think that fear is something to be ashamed of. Amram tries to be funny: "It's like a movie." Jonathan has one major concern: "Do you think we'll have school tomorrow?"

"No, I would think not."

"Oh, boy!"

At least someone is happy with this war.

Why are we not more frightened? We are apprehensive, yes, but not to the extent I would have expected. There are no manifestations of real fear. It is all so unreal, so dream-like.

A huge explosion nearby. The ground trembles. Showers of flame leap up, die out. The iron shelter door springs open from the shock and creaks idly to and fro.

"Glad we are so well-protected," mumbles a female voice.

"Katzenelenbogen is right. He's safer in the apartment," says another.

"If a bomb ever hit we'd all be buried alive down here. This is a tomb for the living."

So, everyone is now getting edgy. Some of the younger children begin to sob. I pull Reuven aside and ask him quietly if there is an alternate exit if the door is ever blocked by debris. (Reuven is the Talmud student who is an absolute genius in things mechanical.) There is no other way out except for the small trap door in the rear of the shelter, and that can easily be blocked. We decide on a method to dig our way out if necessary. And we get busy trying to repair the swinging entrance door.

There is still no solid news from the war fronts. We hear only what the enemy is doing to us, and he seems to be attacking on all sides. Raanana has been shelled, and Tel Baruch on the coast, and Lod Airport — all within a few miles of us. But friend Emek Peri sounds reassuring as always. He says very little, but exudes confidence. He calms, comforts, soothes our nerves. We do catch one phrase which is encouraging: "We are fighting on the soil of the enemy." But someone should inform Emek that the enemy is shelling our soil.

Reuven has dashed up into his apartment to get an axe — just in case we have to crack into some walls. He returns dejected. "I just got the BBC on my big radio. They report that the U.S. State Department says that America is remaining neutral in thought, word, and deed."

Is it my imagination, or does everyone in the shelter turn to look at me? Am I responsible for what our State Department does? Neutral! I try to pass it off as a false rumor, as a report that the Arabs are spreading. But I am not convinced and, in the midst of the shelling, neither are they.

At eleven o'clock the all-clear sounds. Finally. We trudge up through the blacked-out halls into our apartment and fall into bed, spent and exhausted. We all decide to sleep in our clothes, since we don't expect to sleep very long in any case. The children, for the first time in their lives, voluntarily line up their shoes and socks at the foot of their beds. They want to be able to find them at the next alarm. Amram wants to sleep with me and Chavah with Estelle. Before closing my eyes I idly turn the radio dial and come across an English language propaganda broadcast on Radio Cairo. An announcer with a heavy German accent is screaming at us: "We are coming! Forty million Arabs are coming to liberate our Palestine homeland! You had all better leave. Dayan and Rabin have already escaped. Eshkol is in Greece. Your army has been routed, your air force is destroyed. We are coming, we are coming!" It sounds like a "Sky Is Falling" script, but it is real. Of course I know he is exaggerating, but I have trouble falling asleep after that. Personally, I prefer Emek Peri.

27 Iyar

Tuesday, June 6

SHEINFELD WAS PARTLY RIGHT about those Arab pilots. From eleven P.M. to four A.M. there are no alerts. But at four, just at daybreak, we are shaken from a deep sleep by that terrifying scream. I groan, and run in to wake the boys, but they are already dressed and cheerfully getting ready to go down to the shelter.

The shelter is filled with the same people, but everyone is in fine mood today, animated, friendly, alive. Israelis by nature are very reserved, almost aloof, but some of our neighbors — even the ladies — who scarcely nodded to us for the past ten months are suddenly friendly.

How things have changed. Pious women in Bnei Brak never talk to men, even to men from the neighborhood or from their apartment building whom they may recognize. I remember that during my first weeks here I automatically greeted with a bright hello the lady who lives on the

147

same floor in the next apartment. She looked startled and did not reply. I was taken aback and felt snubbed. But then I decided it was because I had used English which she surely did not understand. The next morning on the steps I gave her a bright and cheerful *Shalom*. She walked past again without the slightest acknowledgement. I realized then that in Bnei Brak a man simply does not speak to another man's wife. It is considered impolite, impious, bad form. Since then, I consciously withheld any greetings to women I may have recognized. I strode past as if they did not exist. A difficult feeling at first — particularly for a Sisterhood-oriented American rabbi — but you get used to it. And now these same women acknowledge my greetings. What wonders hath war wrought.

The news on the radio now is incredible: Israel is claiming the destruction of 375 Arab planes. 375! Incredible, astounding, unbelievable. It cannot be. Undoubtedly this is just an exaggerated war claim. And yet the Israeli Army is not known to make idle claims. 375 planes? Is it possible?

Jerusalem is still being heavily shelled and our troops have invaded the Old City. Good. There is news that we have captured Latrun and Nabi Samuel and are moving to surround the Old City. And El Arish in the Sinai has been captured and we are moving on Aza. So things are not going badly.

Estelle wonders what we will do for food today. We are out of milk, there is just a little bread, and the stores will undoubtedly not be open. As for the milkman, we are lucky if he shows up in normal times. But we will manage.

All is quiet. We hear no sound of anti-aircraft guns, no explosions. The all-clear sounds at five A.M. and the men decide to go to Itchkovitch for *Shacharis*. There is already a large crowd there, overflowing into the street, and everyone is whispering excitedly about the 375 planes. The prevailing opinion is that we have won some important air battles, but that the Air Force has stretched the truth this time in its claims. I pick up BBC on my radio and the announcer is saying, "There are conflicting claims on both sides. Israel claims to have destroyed over 300 Arab planes, while the Arabs are claiming that they have shot down over 200 Israeli aircraft."

An interesting occurrence during *Shacharis*: we are davening out on the sidewalk in typical Itchkovitch fashion, and the *Kohanim* are about to begin their Priestly Blessing. At that moment the air-raid alert sounds again. We all look at one another, no one moves, and without a word or a motion we agree intuitively that we will continue davening and not run to a shelter in the middle of prayer. And so, as the siren continues to wail, the *Kohanim* take their customary position up front, raise their *talleisim* over their heads, cover their faces, stretch forth their arms, the *chazan* intones, "*Kohanim*," and, as if in musical harmony with the alarm, they recite *Birkas Kohanim*, "*Yevarechecha* — May Hashem bless you and keep you. May Hashem turn His countenance upon you and be gracious unto you. May Hashem turn His countenance unto you and give you —" and just as they are about to utter the last word of the blessing — "*Shalom*, peace" — the all-clear sounds and they chant *Shalom* in counterpoint to the siren.

It is just before six A.M. We are back in the shelter waiting for the next all-clear when we hear the clip-clop of a horse and the clinking of glass. We dash out of the shelter and there, resplendent with his white bottles, is our milkman.

Our milkman: how we used to curse him silently every morning, him and his creaking wagon and neighing horse and noisy bottles. How could he be so coarse, so insensitive, so oblivious to the fact that it was still nighttime and we were asleep? And how we used to resent the fact that the bottoms of the bottles were always encrusted with mud and sand. Milkman, all is forgiven: we surround him and chatter gaily and the children jump up and down and embrace him and climb up on his dreary, gray horse.

It occurs to me suddenly that our family in the U.S. must be frantic, and I go over to the post office to send a telegram. There is a long line in front of the telegraph clerk. He seems to be discussing the wording of every telegram presented to him. Perhaps there is an emergency limit on the amount of words, or maybe a special censorship has been imposed. As I get closer to him I can hear what he is doing.

'What?" he says. "You are telling them that there is still some danger? Change that. We are not in danger."

Dutifully the customer makes the appropriate correction.

"*Oy*," he says to the next man. "Why do you have to mention about the shelling? The shelling was nothing. You should have seen Europe. Just take that part out."

"Ah," he beams at a lady's text, "*this* is the kind of telegram to send. Everybody listen. This is a model. ENEMY IS DEFEATED. ALL ARE WELL. GOD HAS REVEALED HIMSELF TO ISRAEL. DO NOT WORRY. That's what a telegram should be: encouraging, happy. We have to show the outside world that we are the victors."

So it goes. He edits and deletes and rewrites and censors — a word here, a phrase there. If the outside world this morning is receiving unusually ecstatic messages from a country at war, they have this clerk to thank.

Things are quiet. It is nine A.M. I decide to drive over to the university and see what has happened there. Who knows, the stiff upper-lippers may have decided to hold classes as always. But except for army personnel, Bar Ilan is almost completely deserted. On the way home, I pick up two hitchhikers, and as we cruise along, the air alert screams again. I am not far from home and we decide to continue on. On the road we see a woman scurrying along. There is no shelter in sight, no buildings, only open fields. I pull up quickly beside her and tell her to jump in the back and I will take her to a shelter. She opens up the back door, stares inside, but does not budge. Then I remember: there is no seat in the back. I had removed it completely last week, during my post office duties, to make room for the bulky packages we were delivering. The siren is still wailing, we are all alone on the highway. I urge her to climb in quickly and to sit on the floor. She slams the door in a huff.

"Crouch down like a monkey? Not me."

"But you are in danger. You'll only be uncomfortable for a few moments."

"No, no," she says angrily. "You just go on. I will walk, I will walk. Just go on." And off she goes.

The news reports continue to be good. The Arab armies are apparently in retreat in the Sinai. And the fantastic air victory is evidently a fact. Voice of America claims that our paratroopers have taken Sharm el Sheikh, which controls the Straits of Tiran. So it has come true, that song they were singing for the soldiers last week — "*Anachnu naavor* — We will pass through the Straits of Tiran."

Songs: the radio today is no longer concentrating on martial music, but rather on old, nostalgic melodies about Palestine and the kibbutzim and the Bible — the songs we used to sing as children when Israel was a pipe dream. One song is constantly repeated, and this is that new one which was just written a month ago. *Yerushalayim shel zahav* — Jerusalem of Gold. Amazing how it has caught on. It is a sad, longing, plaintive, tearful, sentimental melody, and the words are charged with emotion.

> Jerusalem of Gold
> And of copper and of light,
> For all your songs I am the accompanying harp.
>
> In the quiet of tree and rock,
> Deep in her dream,
> The city sits alone,
> And within her is a Wall.
>
> How have the water-springs dried up,
> The crowded market become empty,
> No one visits the Temple Mount
> In the Old City.

In any other time, I suppose the song would be considered rather maudlin, but right now it is sweeping the country. It expresses the kind of sentimentality and emotionalism which lurks beneath the harsh exterior of the Israelis. The song was recorded last week in the Sinai, sung for the troops, and in the background one can hear the soldiers themselves helping along in their rough, rasping voices. It is magnificent.

I have been exposed to an entire Hebrew military vocabulary during these past thirty-six hours — words I never knew existed. *Ptzatzah*-bomb; *krav*-battle; *ippul*-blackout; *shirion*-tank; *miklat*-shelter; *azakah*-alarm; *hargaah*-all-clear; *tsalafim*-snipers; *pagaz*-shell.

There are also more familiar words. Artillery is *artilleria*; tanks are *tankim*; jeeps are *jippim*; command-car is *command-car*.

As the afternoon fades into dusk, we live from one news broadcast to the next. It is clear that we are closing in on Jerusalem. And from the South comes more good news. Rafiah on the Gaza Strip is in our hands, as are El-Arish, Abu-Ageila, Gevel-Livni. The names are beautiful, melodic, sweet. We savor them, and they linger like soft wine on the palate. *El-Arish, Gevel-Livni, Rafiah.* We tack up our large area map on the living room wall and whenever the radio announces the capture of another city we circle it in red, and we follow our advance on all fronts.

There are reports that we have destroyed two hundred Egyptian tanks, and that their army is en route back towards Suez. Thousands of Egyptian prisoners are being captured.

In today's paper is a photograph of a single Israeli soldier with a gun guarding about five hundred Egyptian prisoners, and the mind moves back two weeks when we read the Torah portion in *Vayikra* 26: "You will pursue your enemies, and they will fall before your sword, and five among you will pursue a hundred, and a hundred will pursue ten thousand." And the mind moves back twenty years and I recall the famous photograph of hundreds of terrified Jews marching down a European street in front of a single German soldier with a gun. That lone Israeli soldier: chances are that his mother and father were burned in Auschwitz. In twenty years the captives have become the captors, the oppressors have become the victims, the conquered have become the conquerors, the defeated have become the victors.

There is one other difference between those two photographs. Those Arab prisoners are not being sent to gas chambers; instead they are being given food and water by the Israelis, and there is already talk of repatriating them back to Egypt.

Arab radio — particularly Radio Cairo — has become a great source of entertainment for all of us. They are claiming smashing victories.

"Soldiers of Israel," they shout, "your homes are destroyed. Your women have been taken, your children are captured. Tel Aviv is in flames, Haifa is burning, Jerusalem is overrun."

It has the dramatic cadence of a Biblical text, but it is nevertheless very amusing. There follows a rousing marching song and another commercial.

"Mothers and children of Israel. Your husbands are no longer. Your armies have taken flight, your dead are strewn all over the fields of battle. We have taken Tiberias and are approaching Nazareth and Haifa. We are coming. Forty million Arabs are coming to liberate our homeland."

More music. Then an attack on Dayan: "He has lost one eye. We are going to knock out the other eye. We are coming."

I ask Sheinfeld why, with such a victory at hand, the Israelis are not dancing in the streets. He shrugs his shoulders.

"There are *korbanot*, sacrifices," he says. "When you read our casualty lists you won't feel like dancing."

At Itchkovitch this evening, Schwab is excitedly saying, "You see, I told you we had a secret weapon. One hundred rockets a second from an underground silo."

Someone taps him on the shoulder. "Schwab," he says quietly, "our secret weapon is up there." And he points to the sky.

And it is true. As more news comes tumbling in of the rout of the Arab armies, there is a feeling in the air of something supernatural. We are as if in a trance. We are awake, we are aware, we are conscious, but it is all unreal, so much like a dream. The fear and the tension of the last week, the bombardment of yesterday, the dark shelter — and now today's giddy sense of sudden triumph. We walk on air in a kind of euphoria, we are intoxicated. We are afraid to utter the word, we are afraid to think that we have been worthy of it. *Ness* is the word: miracle. Have we, the generation of Dachau and Auschwitz, been witness to a miracle? Have we seen the *Shechinah*, the presence of God? Is it possible that our outnumbered, outmanned army of clerks and students and accountants has routed six Egyptian divisions and nine hundred tanks and four hundred planes — all in a few hours? And that we are in the Old City of Jerusalem?

What else but a miracle? But a miracle for us? Why were we, among all the generations, found worthy of a miracle?

Surely it is not for us alone that God has ceased to hide His face. Surely it was for the six million whose souls expired through the black chimneys of Maidenek and Treblinka that Hashem of the universe, twenty years later, chose Israel, His Holy Land, as the place upon which He would again reveal Himself as the Living God of Israel.

Officially no one is allowed to be on the streets at night during the blackout, but Estelle and I go out for a half-hour stroll just to unwind. The total quiet is unreal, yet how lovely the night sky is. Must human beings lock themselves behind blackout shades before we can see the night sky? What is it about a star that refuses to reveal itself to men while they stand among lights, and no sooner do men's lights disappear than the stars allow themselves to be viewed? Not a sound on the streets, and it is only eight o'clock. Here and there, the muted sounds of an air-raid warden's footsteps and the swinging blue light of his lantern, and the rest is black and silent.

28 Iyar

Wednesday, June 7

HOW BRIGHT AND BLUE are this morning's heavens, as bright as the day's news. Victories on all fronts, new cities and towns captured, names I never heard of. Our soldiers are on the way to Suez at an even faster pace than in 1956. Shechem has surrendered, and Jerusalem will soon be ours again.

It is mid-afternoon and we get the word. It is ours. The Temple Mount, the Western Wall, the entire Old City of Jerusalem is ours. Prayers have already been held at the Wall by the Chief Chaplain and by our troops. It is ours. It is a dream.

Special editions of the newspapers have hit the streets and been gobbled up. They have these headlines: THE WALL IS AGAIN OURS. And, THE PLACE FOR WHICH WE HAVE WAITED 2000 YEARS. *Yediot Aharonot*, hardly a religious newspaper, carries on its masthead a quotation from *Yeshayahu* 52:9, "Break forth in song, shout together, O ruins of Jerusalem; Hashem has comforted His people, He has redeemed Jerusalem." Other newspapers feature similar passages, such as *Tehillim* 122: "Our feet stood within your gates, O Jerusalem. The built-up Jerusalem is like a city that is united together."

During the evening there is a radio broadcast from the Wall. We hear the Chief Chaplain read a memorial prayer for the fallen, the *Kaddish* is recited, in the background is the sound of shooting, the soldiers chant lustily the ancient blessing of "*Shehecheyanu* — Who has kept us in life, and sustained us, and allowed us to attain this moment." It is a two thousand-year-old blessing. They sound the shofar: *tekiah*, *shevarim*, *teruah*, over and over again. The soldiers at the Wall fall into each other's arms and weep. The announcer weeps. And we weep, together with all of Israel. Throughout the evening that program is played and replayed, again and again, and each time we weep anew. Jewish rule over the Old City — for the first time in two thousand years.

It will take time for this to penetrate. We are numb, without words and without expression. I think of *Tehillim* 126: "When God returned the captivity of Tzion, we were as dreamers."

After *Shacharis*, the *chazan* begins to chant *Tehillim* 83, as we have been doing since May 20. But he is interrupted by an angry shout. An old bearded man comes forward.

"No, no more *Tehillim*. Enough. We have won, have we not? Let us not bother God with pleas now. Everything in *Tehillim* 83 has been fulfilled. We have won. I say, let us say *Hallel* — let us praise God, and thank Him. Today is for joy, not for tears."

There is total confusion, arguments, shouting. Finally, there is a compromise. They recite the chapter in *Tehillim*, and those who wish to remain later recite the *Hallel* as well. Discord has returned; the war is over.

29 Iyar

Thursday, June 8

WHY IS THERE NO news from the Syrian front? This is very disquieting. Radio Damascus is still making wild claims about the capture of Israeli cities in the northern Galilee, and while everyone knows that these are lies, the fact that the Israelis have not given out the slightest news about our own action is making us somewhat nervous. There is a universal hope here, however, that Syria will not accept any cease-fire proposals from the U.N. before Israel has a chance to hit her hard.

Syria is, after all, the underlying cause of most of our trouble, and we consider her to be far more meddlesome and extreme than Egypt.

Item in today's paper: the Israeli government is arranging a trip for foreign correspondents to the Old City tomorrow. Since Adolph Rosenberg, publisher of our *Southern*

Israelite, is in Tel Aviv, I decide to ask him to get the proper credentials for me. During the drive through Tel Aviv, I idly turn on the radio and get Radio Cairo. Tel Aviv, I learn, is burning. They repeat this news item every three minutes. I look around me and all is peaceful in Tel Aviv. An odd, unreal feeling.

Adolph is staying at the Tel Aviv Hilton. There is only one thing wrong with Hilton hotels. The decor may be native, but it is all too, too American. Tel Aviv or Cairo or Ankara or New York — a Hilton by any other name…

Adolph is extremely helpful and after several telephone calls I become a fully accredited foreign correspondent and am signed up for tomorrow's trip to the Old City, the Western Wall, and Bethlehem. Just three nights ago I was jesting about davening at the Wall — and now tomorrow!

Downstairs in the lobby I meet an American lady, a leader of a women's Zionist group in New York, who had to come to Israel on one of those ubiquitous "study mission" junkets, and was unable to book passage back to the States prior to the war. She had just come in from swimming and sunbathing.

"My heavens," she whines, "this war is just ruining my vacation."

1 Sivan

Friday, June 9

THIS MORNING IS THE morning. Together with the foreign correspondents I visit the *Ir Ha'atikah* — the Old City of Jerusalem. That slides off the pen so easily: I visit the *Ir Ha'atikah*. Best for now not to dwell on the unreality of it all and the choking anticipation as we drive towards the ancient city walls.

We walk through Damascus Gate and the narrow winding streets. From every window flutters a white flag. The Arabs crouching on their stoops eye us with a mixture of hostility and curiosity. We walk towards the Temple Mount and the gold-domed Mosque of Omar, which is built right on the spot where the Holy of Holies of the *Beis Hamikdash* stood. (I will not try to describe my feelings.) Through a huge, wooden gate, down some steps, and there it stands — stark and gray and brooding. The *Kotel Hamaaravi*, the Western Wall, the Wailing Wall, the last vestige of the glory of ancient Israel.

161

How do you embrace a wall? I have seen its picture hundreds of times, and dozens of paintings and sketches, but my eyes have never looked upon it as they do now; I have read poems about it, and short stories and novels, but I have never placed my two hands upon it as I do now; I have studied ancient texts about it, and seen what the Midrash and Chazal say about it, but I have never touched my cheeks against the cool, rough-hewn slabs of limestone as I do now. I want to weep, but I cannot. I can only rest my forehead in its dark crevices and stare, dumb and mute and silent.

Soldiers, grimy and hot from battle, are running up to it, touching the huge blocks of stone, caressing them, prostrating themselves on the ground. They put on *tallis* and *tefillin* and with their guns on their shoulders and in full battle dress they pray and shout out the *Shema* — Hear O Israel, Hashem is our God, Hashem is One.

I notice that everyone takes a scrap of paper, scribbles something on it, and places it between the huge blocks. I do likewise, and write on it the names of the entire family, with a prayer for health. The *Shechinah*, God's presence, say Chazal, hovers over the Wall. Today it hovers over all of Israel.

We go on to visit Bethlehem, only a few miles away. I ask the driver if we can stop at Rachel's Tomb. It is late, but he reluctantly agrees.

"Five-minute stop to visit Rachel's Tomb," he announces.

"I've waited two thousand years and you give us five minutes," I say.

Everyone laughs. But I was not joking.

The Tomb is housed in a small, domed, one-story building. It is crowded with soldiers. Hundreds of lit candles flicker on the walls. The soldiers kiss the Tomb, recite *Tehillim*, close their eyes in thought. A young soldier with beard, *peyos,* and *yarmulke* guards the building outside.

In *Bereishis* 35 is the story of Rachel's burial:

> And Rachel died and was buried on the way to Efrat, which is Bethlehem. And Yaakov made a monument upon her grave, and this is the monument which is on Rachel's grave unto this day.

The prophet Yirmeyahu declares that Rachel constantly weeps for her children who have been driven into exile, unto this day. Rachel, beloved wife of Yaakov, mother of Yosef and Binyamin — Rachel's weeping surely subsided a bit today as her children returned to tiny Bethlehem and crowded around her graveside.

Outside, in Bethlehem's town square, I notice from a distance a young paratrooper patrolling the area. His machine gun looks as big as he is. There is something familiar about him, but his back is turned to me. I come closer. His uniform is caked with dirt, and on his head is a black *yarmulke.* He turns. It is Rachamim. He sees me and runs to me with a shout. We embrace. He had fought his way through Jerusalem and down into Bethlehem. He has changed. In the span of a few weeks he has been transformed into a soldier, erect, proud, tough, darkly tanned. He is a walking arsenal. With his machine gun he has a pistol, two knives, several hand grenades, and a string of bullets strapped to his back and his waist.

But Rachamim does not have war on his mind.

"Tell me," he says with a smile. "Do you really think I am going to fail?"

I stare at him, unable to respond.

"I mean, really," he persists, "you know I was trying very hard. I will study more as soon as I can get home."

"Rachamim," I finally stammer, "you are not going to fail. I am going to give you an A."

Rachamim laughs. He thinks it is a fine joke.

But Rachamim is going to get an A. Not for his work in class, but for his work in saving my life.

We jounce home on the bus and I let my mind wander. For years Jews have been staring across the Jerusalem border at the soft rolling hills, gray and tan and strangely yellow, with a longing and a sadness and a resignation and a sigh. Those hills were "theirs," not ours, although they were really ours and not theirs. The best word for the feeling is the Hebrew *ga'aguim*, a deep longing, an aching desire. We used to look at the border from all sides and angles, from Talpiot and Ramat Rachel at the southern end of Jerusalem, where you could buy a soda and climb up to the roof of the kiosk at the top of a hill and let your eyes follow the road to Bethlehem as it disappeared behind a hill. Beyond the road, you were told, was Rachel's Tomb. Just five minutes away. Five minutes! You would stare at that hill, trying to pierce it with your eye, wondering what was on the other side, what Bethlehem and the Tomb of Rachel really looked like. Or you would look towards the northeast in the direction of Jericho and Shechem; or south towards Hebron, one of the truly old cities in the world. Or you would dash to the Abu Tor overlook, a little farther north, which juts out in a zigzag pattern and places you almost parallel to *Har Habayis* and there you would gaze across the great valley and imagine that you saw the Wailing Wall near the Dome of the Rock, the Mosque of Omar; or you would climb *Har Tzion*, the closest vantage point of all, where you would rent a pair of binoculars and climb the minaret atop the hill and get a good look at the Mount of Olives and the winding roads and paths that lace the ochre hills in the distance.

What will happen now to the binocular vendor on *Har Tzion*, and to the ice-cream vendor at Ramat Rachel? Casualties of the war.

I get home just before Shabbos begins, change my clothes, and dash off to shul. When I walk in I realize that everyone has already heard that I have been at the Wall. Suddenly I am a celebrity. They crowd around me.

"What is it like?"

"Were you there?"

"Did you touch it?"

"Is it damaged?"

"Was it crowded?"

"Tell us about it."

"Can you take us there, too?"

Mercifully, the prayers begin. But tonight there is one American Jew who is the envy of all of Bnei Brak.

During davening I notice new posters on the shul wall.

TO OUR BRETHREN THE CHILDREN OF ISRAEL
WHEREVER THEY MAY BE FOUND:

This week we have seen the hand of God. The first half of the passage in *Vayikra* 26:12 has been fulfilled, "And I will walk in your midst, and I will be unto You, Hashem." God has fulfilled His promise, but only we can fulfill the second half of that same passage: "…and you will be unto Me for a people." If we are to be God's people, we must acknowledge His miraculous deliverance and we must turn to Him with all our heart, with all our soul, and with all our might.

The war may be over, but the rabbis are still on the front lines of the wars of Hashem.

But the war is hardly over. First of all, the wounded are being brought back home, the casualty lists contain hundreds of dead, and the reality of the bloodletting is doing more than anything else to bring us all back to earth. We are still ecstatic, but we are beginning to realize the terrible cost.

Nor is the war over physically. All of last night and this morning hundreds of planes have been streaking northward, wave after wave of them. I did not realize Israel owned so much aircraft. Obviously, there is an all-out attack on the Syrian fortifications. This will be bloody.

An overpowering God-consciousness is apparently sweeping Israel. There are reports that in Tel Aviv and other cities people have been standing in line to buy *siddurim* and *tefillin* and *tzitzis*. Somehow there is a desire to express something to God, and for this purpose Jews automatically revert to the ancient forms. This is a deeply emotional and religious moment in the history of the Jewish people, and at such moments the categories of the secular world are simply not adequate.

Amazing stories are filtering back from the war fronts, and even those Israelis who like to think of themselves as secularists are referring unabashedly to miracles. Naturally, all the soldiers prayed before going into battle, but this is in itself not surprising, or miraculous. What is different about all this is the feeling among the tough, hardened veterans of many campaigns that something supernatural has occurred. Everyone is speaking and thinking in terms of Messianic days, and of the fulfillment of prophecy. Some newspapers are even running a daily series of battlefront stories that can only be described as miraculous. The wellsprings of Jewish religious feeling have obviously not dried up.

These are great, historic days we are living through. It seems a pity that the ordinary, mundane aspects of life still have to be attended to: shopping, eating, paying bills, packing, letter-writing, sleeping. There should be, at least for these days, a different manner of living, a manner more spiritual, less ordinary and less mortal. There is a certain strangeness within us. It is the soul which, having suddenly sensed the presence of God in this world, is stirring mightily to release itself from the confines of the body.

And there should be a manner of writing that is more suited to the subject. This is a time for poets and prophets, not for journalists or diarists. The inadequacy of words.

They are beginning to seep into my bones, the recent events, and I find it difficult to write at all.

New cities, with soft and melodic sounds, have entered the language during this week. Strange places, exotic and mysterious: El-Arish, Sharm el Sheikh, Jevel-Livni, Abu Ageila, Jenine, Rafiah, Ishmailiya. Soft sounds, redolent with the warm wind of the desert, the brilliant blazing sun, the sere, shifting sands, the hush and quiet and vast silence of the wilderness of Sinai whose lone and level sands stretch far away.

Many new names, but only one name. Yerushalayim. Yerushalayim, the eternal, the holy, the golden, the City of David, *neveh tzedek, ir shalem, Ariel*. Yerushalayim: the name itself is a melody, a delicate cadence of five shimmering syllables. Have you ever whispered Yerushalayim? How softly, how like the oil from the Mount of Olives does it flow from the lips.

(When the very first Jewish soldiers fought their way through the walls of the Old City, through the Dung Gate, a band of twelve soldiers was sent up the winding path to the *Kotel Hamaaravi*, the Western Wall. When they arrived at the Wall, they found three Jews praying there, completely wrapped in their *tallis* and *tefillin*. The soldiers were stunned.

The sergeant said to them, "How did you get here? We are the first Jews to set foot on these grounds. You could have been killed."

The others replied, "We simply wanted to pray at the Wall."

The sergeant replied, "It is still dangerous. I'm going to get you out of here. We will be right back." And he and his men moved on.

The sergeant returned with the captain moments later. But the three men were no longer there.)

High above the Wall, higher even than *Har Habayis*, is *Har Hazeisim*, the Mount of Olives. From the slopes of *Har Hazeisim* you view the land of Israel: Down to Jericho and the Jordan and the Dead Sea to the east; the flowing hills of Judea to the north and south; and to the west, almost directly below, *Har Habayis*, the sudden flat plateau tucked like a diamond into the hills.

Har Habayis was once *Har Hamoriah*, where Avraham heard the voice of the messenger of God calling, "Avraham, Avraham," and Avraham's hand was stayed and he did not sacrifice his son, his only son whom he loved, Yitzchak. And on this place God blessed Avraham and Yitzchak, and He blessed their seed for all time. And God chose this place for His Holy Temple, for this was the center of His world and the Holy of Holies was the center of the Temple. Here the *Kohen Gadol* officiated; here the Sanhedrin sat in the *Azarah* courtyard; here the *Levi'im* sang their songs on the steps leading up to the *Heichal*, the main building of the *Beis Hamikdash*; here the *Yisraelim*, flowing up from Dan and Beer Sheba and Yaffa and Hebron, came on Pesach and Shavuos and Succos, and they offered up their offerings of thanksgiving and praise to Hashem, the God of Israel.

The soldiers of Israel are still streaming up to their Temple Mount and their Wall. Their faces aglow, they cast their eyes upward and gaze in disbelief at the Wall. As if in a dream they approach it, touch the stones, kiss them. A spontaneous *minyan* begins, a table laden with *tefillin* and *talleisim* appears, and there they stand, the soldiers of Israel, in the olive and tan and yellow of their battle dress, their netted helmets, their automatic rifles slung over their shoulders, dusty and grimy and red-eyed from battle, there they stand, the soldiers of Israel, with *tefillin* beneath their helmets, with the woolen *tallis* covering up the knife hanging from the belt, and the barrel of the gun peeking out from beneath the swaying *tzitzis*.

Some of the soldiers have forgotten how to put on their *tefillin*, some have never known how. But they wind the leather straps onto their arms, awkwardly at first, but proudly, and their buddies who know help them out tenderly and some put the *shel rosh* on top of the helmet, and there they stand, the gentle and fierce young soldiers of Israel at the Western Wall, the Wailing Wall, at the Temple Mount, near the Holy of Holies, and their guns and their helmets and their olive and tan and yellow battle dress and their *tefillin* and their black-and-white *tallis* swaying gently to and fro, there they stand, caressing the stones, weeping without shame, and they shout *Shema Yisrael* and the words reverberate along the Wall and echo across the rolling hills beyond and they say, "Return us to Tzion in mercy," and they cry and touch the stones again in disbelief, the tough young soldiers of Israel at the ancient Wall of *Har Habayis*.

It was the twenty-eighth day of Iyar 5727 when the soldiers of Israel, armed with machine guns and rifles, stood before the *Kotel Hamaaravi* for the first time in two thousand years.

Shout for joy and sing together
Ye ruins of Jerusalem;
For God has comforted His people
He has redeemed Jerusalem.

It was the forty-third day of the *Omer* when the soldiers of Israel, armed with *tallis* and *tefillin*, stood inside the walls of the *Ir Ha'atikah*, the Old City.

Like a mighty hero will God go forth
Like a warrior will He kindle His wrath
He will exult and shout loudly
Over His enemies will He triumph.

It was seven days before the festival of Shavuos when the soldiers of Israel, their gun barrels peeking out beneath their swaying *talleisim*, exulted and shouted loudly as they stood beside the Temple Mount.

And you shall keep the festival of Shavuos
unto Hashem your God
according as Hashem your God blesses you.
And you shall rejoice before Hashem your God:
you and your son and your daughter
and your man-servant and your maidservant
and the *Levi* who is within your gates
and the stranger and the fatherless
and the widow that are in the midst of you
in the place which Hashem your God shall choose
to cause His name to dwell there...

We are as dreamers. God has reached down and touched us on the fingertips — shall we not be as dreamers? I have seen *Har Habayis*, I have touched the *Kotel Hamaaravi*, I have walked in Bethlehem — how can I ever be I again?

The names of the cities we are now holding, are these real? Haunting names, old and hoary and reverent — are they now really ours? Jericho, Bethlehem, Hebron, Shechem, Gaza. The radio says they are ours. The papers show Jewish soldiers standing there, the photographs show our flag waving overhead. Is Jericho really ours? Are there Jewish soldiers in Bethlehem? Does our flag really fly over Hebron, the burial place of Adam and Chavah, and Avraham and Sarah, and Yitzchak and Rivkah, and Yaakov and Leah? Or am I imagining?

So many new names, with soft and melodic sounds. But only one new name, and one soft sound. Yerushalayim, the holy, the golden, the City of David. Have you ever whispered Yerushalayim? Five shimmering syllables. How softly, how like the oil of the Mount of Olives does it flow from the lips, from the lips of dreamers.

When Hashem returns the captivity of Tzion
we shall be like dreamers.
Our mouth will be filled with laughter
and our tongue with singing.
Then shall they say among the nations,
great things has Hashem done for them.
Great things has Hashem done for us,
we shall be joyful.
Bring back again, O Lord, our captivity
like rivulets in arid land.
They who sow in tears
shall reap with joyous song.
He goes forth and weeps,
who bears the seed for sowing,
But he will surely return with joyous song
bearing his sheaves.

Glossary

ABBA: father

ADON: sir, mister

ARON KODESH: Holy Ark which houses the synagogue's Torah Scrolls

AVINU MALKEINU: lit., "our Father, our King"; special prayer recited on fast days and during times of peril

BEIS HAMIKDASH: Holy Temple in Jerusalem

BEIS MIDRASH: Torah study hall

BEKESHE: CHASSIDIC caftan

BEMIDBAR: Numbers

BEREISHIS: Genesis

BIRKAS HAMAZON: Grace after Meals

BRIS: circumcision

B'SEDER: in good order

BOBBE: grandmother

CHALLAH: kneaded bread eaten on Sabbath and holidays

CHASSIDIC: associated with CHASSIDIM

CHASSIDIM: followers of the teachings of the Baal Shem Tov, known for their piety and fervor

CHAZAN: one who leads the prayers

DAAS TORAH: Torah viewpoint

DAVEN: pray

DEVARIM: Deuteronomy

EREV: the eve of

GABBAI: sexton

GALUS: exile

HAGANAH: the Jewish defense forces in Palestine prior to the establishment of the State of Israel

HALLEL: prayers of praise from Psalms recited on holidays and the new moon

HAR: Mount

HAR HABAYIS: the Temple Mount

IR HA'ATIKAH: the Old City

IYOV: Job

KABBALAH: Jewish mysticism

KAPOTTE: caftan

KADDISH: the mourner's prayer

KAVANAH: concentration, sincerity

KIDDUSH: special blessing recited on Sabbaths and holidays

KIDDUSH HASHEM: sanctification of God's Name; self-sacrifice

KOHANIM: pl. for KOHEN

KOHEN: Jew who is a direct descendant of Aaron, brother of Moses

KOL HAKAVOD: lit., "all the honor"; more power to you

KOTEL HAMAARAVI: the Western Wall

KRECHTZ: sigh

LAG BA'OMER: thirty-third day of the OMER, a Jewish day of celebration

LEVI'IM: Levites

LIRA: former Israeli currency (later replaced by the shekel)

LIROT: pl. for LIRA

MAARIV: evening prayer service

MASHIACH: the Messiah

MATZOS: unleavened bread

MECHITZAH: partition separating men and women in a synagogue

MELO KOL HAARETZ KEVODO: "The world is filled with His glory"

MESHUGAAS: idiocy

MIKVEH: ritual pool

MINCHAH: afternoon prayer service

MINYAN: quorum of ten men required for public worship

MITZVAH: Biblical commandment

MITZVOS: pl. for MITZVAH

MOHEL: performer of a BRIS

MOTZA'EI SHABBOS: Saturday night

MUSSAR SHMUESS: ethical discourse

OMER: the seven-week period from the second day of Passover

ORACH CHAIM: one of the four sections of the Jewish *Code of Law*

PESACH: festival of Passover

PEYOS: earlocks

RAV: Rabbi

REB: Rabbi

REBBE: the Rabbinic leader of a CHASSIDIC group

RECHOV: street; boulevard

SHE'EILAH: a question, usually in religious law

SHABBOS: Sabbath

SHACHARIS: morning prayer service

SHALOM ALEICHEM: lit., "peace unto you"; a daily greeting; a Friday night hymn

SHALOSH SEUDOS: the third Sabbath meal

SHAVUOS: festival of Pentecost

SHEITEL: wig worn by Jewish women

SHEKET: quiet

SHTREIMEL: fur hat worn by Chassidic Jews

SHUL: synagogue

SUCCOS: festival of Tabernacles

TALLIS: prayer shawl

TEFILLIN: phylacteries

TEHILLIM: Psalms

TESHUVAH: repentance

TISCH: the Sabbath and holiday table celebration of a REBBE

TZARAH: trouble, crisis, peril

TZITZIS: fringes on the four corners of a TALLIS

VAYIKRA: Leviticus

YARMULKE: skull cap

YECHEZKEL: Ezekiel

YENTE: a combination scatterbrain, gossip, and general nuisance, usually a female

YESHAYAHU: Isaiah

YESHIVA: rabbinical seminary

YIRMEYAHU: Jeremiah

YISRAELIM: a Jew who is not a KOHEN or Levite

ZEMIROS: religious hymns, usually sung at festive meals